# IN THE WORLD

Selected Speeches of
Bettino Craxi

# IN THE WORLD

## Selected Speeches of
## Bettino Craxi

## BETTINO CRAXI

**VANTAGE PRESS**
New York

FIRST EDITION

All rights reserved, including the right of
reproduction in whole or in part in any form.

Copyright © 1996 by Bettino Craxi

Published by Vantage Press, Inc.
516 West 34th Street, New York, New York 10001

Manufactured in the United States of America
ISBN: 0-533-11578-7

Library of Congress Catalog Card No.: 95-90456

0 9 8 7 6 5 4 3 2 1

# Contents

| | |
|---|---:|
| Addis Ababa, 4 July 1990 | 1 |
| LDC Debt Geneva, 7 July 1990 | 9 |
| World Conference on the Less Poor Countries | |
|     Paris, 4 September 1990 | 23 |
| Getting Out of the Debt Crisis Back on the Path of Development | |
|     UNO General Assembly New York, 23 October 1990 | 31 |
| Statement Made by Craxi Rome, 26 October 1990 | 41 |
| Conference on Cooperation for Development | |
|     Rome, 17 October 1991 | 45 |
| Development in Africa: A Commitment of Common Interest | |
|     New York, 28 October 1991 | 53 |
| European Parliament Seminar: The Role of the UN in | |
|     Promoting Development in the World Rome, 28 May 1992 | 63 |
| Report on the Developing Countries' Debt and Growth | 81 |

# IN THE WORLD

Selected Speeches of
Bettino Craxi

# Addis Ababa, 4 July 1990

The African debt—about $250 billion—is structured into two parts roughly amounting to $105 billion in Mediterranean Africa and to about $145 billion in sub-Saharan Africa. Within the international community—for various reasons—the attention given to these debts has been too little, or at any rate, insufficient.

The Mediterranean countries are officially classified as average-income countries, in that they exceed $500 per capita and that their income is less than $600 in Egypt, a little more than $600 in Morocco, about $1,200 in Tunisia and $2,700 in Algeria and probably in Libya as well.

Among these, Egypt, Morocco, and Tunisia belong to a category of countries with an income that stands somewhere between $500 and $1,300—and which should be defined as "intermediary": between the countries that are generally classified as poor and the countries with an average income. The Group of Seven should acknowledge the existence of this category, by differentiating it from the average-income countries, so as to carry out the strategy of debt limitation and allow new financial means, with an eye to economic and social growth.

In sub-Saharan Africa, too, some countries exceeding $500 per capita are being separated from those classified as poor to be included in the average-income category. In reality, these are intermediary countries whose average income is only slightly above the vital minimum.

Many official institutions have expressed their worries about the debt in Africa. The category of intermediary countries deserves particular attention, and it is now very clear that it is necessary to extend the list of countries benefitting from the Toronto Plan and to include further needs in the project; moreover, these very specific considerations on behalf of the IFI countries made through concessionary agencies (Monetary Fund and World Bank) also lead one to think harder in terms of aid policies for development.

The issue related to the debts and development of the Mediterranean African countries are a problem of common interest for both Europe and Africa. It would be very useful to have a regional bank for development, which would operate after the manner of the Inter-American Bank for Development and the Overseas-Development Corporation of Japan, in order to direct new financial resources to these countries with a view to allow productive investments and to support, through insurance and cofinancing guarantees, investments in infrastructures.

For average-income countries, such as Algeria and Libya, the problem is above all one that has to do with new expenses and with the carrying out of innovative financing formulas—which are very different from the traditional type of loans—on behalf of public insurances and banks of industrial countries (especially European countries).

There are other additional problems, which concern more particularly the other countries.

It is necessary to reduce the high cost of interest, which encumbers them, by adapting it to their real paying capacity.

Overall, it would be necessary to carry out a substantial reduction on public accounts receivable, or on any of these involving bilateral public guarantee, in the intermediary income countries, by postponing dates of payment to thirty years and by diminishing interest rates as far as 60 percent with devolution of a quarter of the residual charge for the environment, human capital development, childhood, and growth. In my opinion, particular attention has to be given to projects related to the environment in the Mediterranean region, as well as to the professional training issue for the immigrants' work force. For what concerns, instead, the sub-Saharan African countries, it has been written that their debt is quite modest—only $16 billion—that their economic weight in international commerce is almost nonexistent, and that the problem of their debt, which is very serious to them, only arouses very little and sporadic attention. In the budgets of the big international banks, their debt is certainly not a problem managers, shareholders and supervising authorities should lose any sleep on.

This conclusion is erroneous, from an economic as well as from an ethical or political viewpoint.

As insignificant as the amount of accounts receivable to reimburse debt may be for rich countries, it turns into a real burden for poor countries. Reimbursement for debt is about 40–50 percent of those countries' budgets.

Much is being said at the present on economic ethics and business ethics. Therefore, in my opinion, ethical thinking on this debt is necessary.

Where public finances are concerned, payment of these interest rates and redemptions implies a sacrifice on primary necessities, a reduction on investment which is already weak, or repercussion on goods and consumption which are already, on average, below survival standards.

With a total payment of interest charges of $4.5 billion, the arrears of sub-Saharan Africa now reaches $3.5 billion. The total amounts to $8 billion: 6.4 percent of the debt's capital, or 2.4 percent net of inflation.

This weight is overwhelming for sub-Saharan African countries. In fact, this sum is higher than the PIB's global growth rate, which is weakly positive, and the growth rate per capita (which is negative).

A great share of the total debt of the sub-Saharan African countries is directly contracted from governments or from their organizations (especially the state insurance organizations of internationl commerce) with the consequent interest charges implied, or from multilateral organizations which apply minimum interest rates.

Another share of the bilateral debt originates in those loans granted by state insurance companies, at normal market interest rates or at higher rates than those applied on the market and which were raised by governments.

The burden of the debt reimbursement has an impact on domestic savings, which, at only 14 percent of the PIB, can already be considered modest.

It has been noticed that "credit organizations for exportation have generally not hesitated to increase enormously their loans to Africa. The remaining balance owed to these organizations is still one of the most critical issues in the sub-Saharan Africa's debt (even if there have been practically no more loans in the past few years), given that most of these loans were granted at very onerous commercial conditions."

Governments of rich countries find themselves face to face with an ethical problem.

In sub-Saharan Africa, the gross domestic product went down 3.1 percent per capita between 1980 and 1986, while consumptions diminished 2.4 percent, and exportations dropped 2.1 percent per year.

Importations fell even more: 7.5 percent per year, with simultaneous cuts in all new investments, maintenance and consumption.

The slenderness of growth also depends on the numerous natural disasters and on the drop in prices of raw materials, which are the largest slice of exportations for these countries. In fact, during the 1980–87 period, the price of coffee went down 30 percent, the price of cotton dropped 32 percent, iron ore dropped 17 percent and oil went down 53 percent.

Owing to loans without security and to bilateral and multilateral aid, the total flow of resources makes up 7.3 percent of the PIB, and only 2.3 percent is the quota devoted to investment. Public deficit being equal to 6 percent of the PIB, the consequence is a worrying decline of the capital accrual from 21 percent to 17.5 percent between the early and late eighties.

Short- and long-term loans with official creditors have become the main source of financing, while medium-term banking credit is being less frequently used.

This latter type of credit could play a much more important role if, for example, it were guaranteed on exportation products and if industrial countries offered an adequate type of insurance.

Between 1985 and 1989, credit coming from the IMF went down $1.5 billion.

The reason for this is simple but tragic.

These countries are unable to pay the reimbursement on the IMF's loans, and consequently the IMF is unable (because of its rules) to grant new loans.

This obstacle prevents them from making use of all the reconstruction plans the IMF has to offer, which do include, for instance, support from the IMF itself. And this leaves out of consideration the manner in which the IMF's conditions are expressed.

The economic problem of the sub-Saharan countries is impossible to solve without making a drastic reduction in their debt and without exceptional conditions on behalf of the IMF and the World Bank as far as grantings go.

It is very important to put together, in a firm manner, reconstruction policies. It is often a matter of carrying out improvements in public returns and eliminating and/or modifying the innumerable regulations of corporate planning and forms of collectivism and paracollectivism, aiming to a strong modernization of the market structures.

Nevertheless, the adjustment process has to be a selective one. We can't possibly ask a country that only lives on bread to increase the price of bread, because we would be gambling lives for a few million dollars more.

More significant concessions must be made.

Working out some way of reducing the debt is the only possible prospect of a solution to allow the sub-Saharan African countries to come out of this vicious circle.

On the total interest rate charged on the debt—which is over $12 billion, gross of arrears—only $2.6 billion (half for interest and half for redemption) goes to multilateral organizations. And $600 million of that amount is for transactions linked to concessions.

It is necessary to make the maximum effort to transform all these debts into loans that would be granted in a long-term period, with a 50 percent reduction of the interest rate.

The interest rate on the $53 billion bilateral credit granted amounts to $4 billion; only one billion has been paid back, and another billion is pure redemptions.

For the poorest—IDA-eligible—countries, according to the opinions expressed by Italy and France, an ethical duty makes it necessary to go about abolishing reimbursement on these loans, by simply charging it to the public budget of each corresponding year.

For what concerns the bilateral credit to non-IDA-eligible poor countries, the best solution would be to come up with loans allowing a forty-year payment term and a very low interest rate of 1 percent, for example; reimbursement of this loan would go to equalization funds, in local index-linked currency, to financing of development projects, as well as other purposes such as safeguarding the environment (the protection of the equatorial forest and the campaign against desertification are primary points) and valorization of human capital. For average-income countries, reductions should be inferior. In the whole, reductions could be planned as follows: $3.2 billion of interest, while the remaining $800 million would go with the redemptions to equalization funds for the above-mentioned purposes.

Banks also have a role to play. On the $16 billion of accounts receivable, they have had an interest and redemption flow of 1.2 billion (net of arrears). We are talking about a 7.5 percent share. A general plan that would establish thirty-year debentures, based on paying capacity, would make us hope to reach a limitation of about $560 million, at 3.5 percent of the annual charge in currency. For countries in more severe situations, reductions should be greater; however, for countries in less urgent situations that have to deal with a charge beyond 3.5 percent, the difference should be deposited in local currencies, in index-linked accounts, likely to be spent for local benefits. A guarantee on credits should render this transaction advantageous in terms of market conditions.

Five billion less in debt reimbursement (3.5 percent of public budgets, for an amount of $700 million each) for multilateral banks and institutions is nothing in the finances of the rich. They mean survival for the poor and they open a door for them to draw more financial means destined for growth, at a 6 percent rate, which is estimated possible and indispensable.

Besides the financial mathematics question, a little room must be made in the name of solidarity, if we wish to avoid the receipts register of the rich countries on poor countries, with all its impressive principles, to appear terribly hypocritical.

# LDC Debt
# Geneva, 7 July 1990

# I

From an interdependence point of view, by looking at the debt of the less developed countries, one realizes the issue doesn't concern solely the debtor countries, their financial public and private institutions, or their people.

The debt is an issue that concerns every single one of us and which could lead the industrialized countries and the multilateral institutions into a "tunnel," all because of the lacking financial innovation and common action, at a time "peace dividends" could bring the best results.

The debt problem we are analyzing is one of responsbility on behalf of the rich regions toward the poor regions; 800 million people live on one side of the planet, and 4 billion people—among these are almost 1 billion, which constitute the oppressed risking to be overwhelmed by the debt—live on the other side.

Almost 70 percent of the world income is produced and spent by 15 percent of the population. Thus, countries of the Third World, which account for 76 percent of the world population, have less than 20 percent of the world income.

Within this segment are the poor countries, which contain a good half of the world population and have only 5.6 percent of the world income.

In 1987, while the per-capita income of the poor countries in the Third World amounted to only $290, that of the advanced countries with market economies amounted to about $14,500, in other words fifty times as much. In 1987, an Ethiopian earned an average of $130, a Swiss earned $21,000: that is 150 times as much.

In the poor countries of Africa, Asia, and South America, the per-capita daily intake of calories is 2,385; in the industrial countries it is 3,375.

Life expectancy is forty-seven years of age in a number of countries of black Africa. In the rich countries of the West, life expectancy is seventy-seven.

Maternal mortality for every single 100,000 inhabitants amounts to 9 mothers in the U.S.A., 1,500 in Nigeria, and 500 in India!

Because of their modest economic development, the so-called developing countries are "nonexistent," compared to the world commerce giants made of the industrialized countries and their multinational corporations.

In 1987, the total of all exportations amounted to $2,390 billion, while importations amounted to $2,470 billion. With their 440 million inhabitants, the sub-Saharan African countries' trade exchange was only 1.5 percent that of the industrialized countries, just a few billion dollars.

For Latin America and the Caribbean (400 million inhabitants), which also stand among the average-income countries, foreign trade was 4 percent of that of the industrialized countries.

This commercial dependence is even more obvious if one considers what is being exported by these countries (mainly primary commodities and materials) and what they import (primarily finished products and high technology).

Thinking about it all, one will understand that the world trade issue is not to be thought of in terms of abstract laissez faire among unequals, but in terms of regional common markets between rich countries and weak countries. The industrialized countries belonging to the G-7 will have to appoint leaders—collectively and each according to its geographical location—to provide for the reconstruction and development needs in Latin America and the Caribbean, Asia, the Mediterranean, sub-Saharan Africa, and now Eastern Europe.

It must not be forgotten that the industrialized countries are being expected to carry out a concrete task in the southern part of the world, while still another issue appears as imminent: helping the collectivistic economies to come out of their isolation and leading them back into the free market.

We must be aware that success on an international scale will lead the industralized countries toward further commitments.

The trend of the real interest rate was a primary element in the issue of the debt of the developing countries. From a level which was often near zero or negative in the seventies, real interest rates went up above 5 percent and even beyond 10 percent in the first half of the eighties. This was caused by the restrictive monetary policies generally adopted in the industrialized countries to compensate for the fiscal policy's deficiencies, and in the case of some of these countries, because of deliberate choices of a deflationary nature, intended—through unemployment—for making drastic cuts in salaries.

## II

The foreign debt of the developing countries is now enormous. It has grown out of proportion between 1980 and 1990.

According to the IMF, the debt has reached almost $1,200 billion. The World Bank's figure is closer to $1,150.

The debt is expected to reach $1,246 billion by 1990.

At the beginning of the decade, the figure was approximately $600 billion.

The flow of payments for interests and amortizations too has gone way up, from approximately $90 billion in 1980 to the current $160, which is expected to turn into $175 in 1990.

It is a question of bonds being handled through the capitalization of arrears owed. Meanwhile, the debt is growing and growing.

It has to be noticed that, essentially, the problem of the foreign debt is a problem of public debt, which the less developed countries have had to face, and which is connected to the budget deficit of the public sector as a whole.

Public investments were not necessarily linked to the foreign debt issue.

At any rate, their profit had to be measured with the cost of this debt: since the interest rate agreed on was, in most cases, a variable rate, its rapid growth made many projects uneconomic.

Besides, the foreign debt was often a means for financing the balance of payments deficit, and it was somehow connected to the deficit of the public sector, in part because of the fall in prices of raw materials, which many developing countries hoped would be only a transitory phenomenon.

The primary cause for the abnormal growth of the foreign debt of the less developed countries is the absence of international rules of monetary and fiscal constitution in this respect. No rule was settled regarding the possibility of issuing international public debt in the unusual bank credit form or in the quite insidious form of variable-rate financing on the international market in foreign currencies with fluctuating exchange rates.

In the seventies, the sudden increase of such procedures was essentially due to the fact that banks, which carried out transactions on the Eurodollar and usually on offshore currencies, all of a sudden found themselves jammed with petrodollars and trapped into a frantic and vicious loaning cycle.

The GIP growth rates of the seriously indebted countries are low compared to those of other LDCs: less than 2 percent between 1983 and 1989 for the first, compared to 6 percent for the second. Exportation shows only a 4.6 percent increase for the first category, but a 10.5 percent growth for the second. Thus, imports in the countries burdened by the debt are decreasing, instead of increasing as is the case in the other LDCs.

In the strongly indebted countries, the foreign debt has two different negative impacts on such a rate of accumulation: first, because of the need to restrain internal demand and therefore domestic investment, in order to generate a surplus in the balance of foreign trade; second, because banks and official institutions show reluctance in granting further credit.

This is how we now have a pathology in which, as I said, both debtors and creditors are being burdened with a series of responsibilities.

There is a way out, but both creditors and debtors have to do their share.

It can't be ignored that certain Asian countries—which in the early eighties had a serious foreign debt—thanks to a high savings rate, contemporary high diversified productive investment, a favourable economic regime, and cautious monetary and fiscal policies, have managed to reduce considerably the burden of this debt. This was achieved by increasing exportation and thanks to the profitability of domestic capital investment, which was reinvested by their brokers on the national markets.

Indeed it is possible to emerge from the debt crisis as well, as long as the public economy and the market economy function correctly, as long as sacrifices are made, and as long as some financial institutions are ready to support this goal.

## III

Until 1983, the less developed countries were beneficiaries of private net transfers of financial resources. But ever since, there's been a drastic inversion of tendencies.

Lately, a negative balance—which amounts to about $10 billion in terms of figures and is much higher in terms of capacity—on the part of the less developed countries towards the rich countries has become more prominent.

Inevitably, a modification of this abnormal situation and the reinstatement of transfers the other way round, make it necessary to go about an increase on the GIP of the quota of aid for development, from the actual 0.35 percent to about 0.75 percent. This increase was stressed by the DAC, in its various meetings—including the one that took place in May of this year—at governmental level. Saudi Arabia's contribution in aid to development is 2.5 percent.

Every 0.1 percent on the actual income of the rich countries—if we take into account the gross product expected for 1991—amounts to $16.5 billion.

A $30 billion capital could be mobilized yearly through concessionary loans.

The Brady Plan would be much more easily put into practice if it could only benefit from a share of this flow of money.

The same is true for new investments.

Flowing of private financing to the developing countries (including East European countries) should be directed towards three types of new currency transactions: (1) financing of projects, (2) financing of commodities, and (3) industrial credit.

The first group of new finance transactions concerns the carrying out of investment projects, which produce an income supervised by brokers of the industrialized countries.

The kinds of investment appearing to be more suitable are the BTO (build transfer operate) and the BOT (build operate transfer). In both cases a foreign agent is provided to manage the investment, but there are other clear advantages: technical-managerial know-how and collaboration with the director and the agent of the (financial) transaction. In normal loans this is not the case.

In this frame of mind, it is important for public insurance companies to accept insuring not only products but also projects.

In the second group of transactions, foreign investors are involved with financing specific exportations from the developing countries' enterprises, and industrial loans are granted to those enterprises of the Third World carrying out exportation activities.

The most interesting of these transactions is that of the merchant banks, particularly used by Japanese agents and which was recently proposed by Japan for particular transactions with Mexican enterprises.

In this case, the service a foreign bank renders to an enterprise from a developing country doesn't only consist in the loan, but also in the technical help aimed at developing an exportable product, and especially in the international trade services. In such a way, even small-dimension enterprises in developing countries are enabled to sell on the large international markets.

Another interesting model is that of the commodities bonds. Even though they provide for repayment of the capital in question as well as payment dividends for the periods of usufruct, these bonds are tied to a realistic parameter by means of a mechanism which can change the value of the capital as well as the shares of stock.

Such a reference mark is usually the price of a "commodity," in other words of a "basic merchandise" or "raw material."

Therefore, it is obvious that mined raw materials are more adequate than others, as they represent a form of guarantee even by remaining in the subsoil.

The third group includes joint ventures between agents from the rich countries and private agents from developing countries, to be financed also through loans, and mixed enterprises comprehending public enterprises of the less developed countries and bigger enterprises of the industrialized countries, as well as real privatizations.

## IV

The results of the Uruguay Round are very unsure. There is the risk of a blockade, which is very worrisome for North-South relations (as well as others). However, it must be acknowledged that some of the difficulties especially perceived for agriculture, for industries of high intensity of activity but low quality, and technological services, all reflect the superficiality of pure generalized laissez-faire remedies. Agricultural markets, in one way or another, must be stabilized. As much as the Common Agricultural Policy of the EEC might be criticized, one must admit that, under its regime, wonderful productivity sprang. Because it proved to be successful, today we should consider reviewing this policy.

Besides, an excessive liberalization of manufactured products without the necessary controls required by a simple principle of respect, in terms of ecological rules and in terms of nonexploitation of labour (which is cheap in the "less developed countries"), can turn into a dangerous race to degradation.

A liberalization of high-technological services is something to hope for and possible to achieve, if the monopolistic powers establish certain control measures on the weak markets of the LDCs.

All this leads one to believe that aiming to develop "common market" regional areas—each organized according to its local requirements and characteristics, and each having its own specific rules—will probably prove to be more successful than seeking a vague type of cosmic free trade.

President Bush's recent plan of areas of free trade between the United States and Mexico seems much more promising—given the extension of the territory in the Caribbean, Latin America, and towards Canada up north—than any hopes set on the Uruguay Round.

Other similar projects should be undertaken or explored and carried out.

The time of the large regional areas is here.

The debt of Latin America, Africa, and Asia will be more easily solved if trade and financial flows are reactivated.

## V

The Brady Plan is a courageous and realistic project: it acknowledges the need to reduce the bank debt and states that a solid public financial intervention is indispensable in doing so.

It also admits that the indebted countries need new incoming money.

But in various contexts it is stated that the Brady Plan is underfunded. Therefore, it is difficult to carry out cuts on the desired quantity and at the desired pace, or to fully attract new sums of money to the countries which have submitted to this plan and are on the way to recovery.

Other countries should follow Japan in its impressive recycling plan, which grants new sums of money at very favourable conditions to the LDCs and facilitates the Brady Plan. Another solution would be to use the special drawing rights of the rich countries to increase their resources.

It is illogical for a large restructuring with guarantees on residual credit not to be positively reflected on the country-risk and therefore on new loans.

At the moment, there is a group of important banks, from various industrial countries, wishing to continue to operate in the developing countries, especially in Latin America and Asia. But it is necessary that the governments of rich countries encourage such a positive attitude by making appropriate bank modifications in their fiscal and accounting systems, in their insurance policies, and in their support for the work carried out by regional banks for development, for which the Overseas Development Corporation of Japan and the Saudi Development Bank are excellent models.

The Toronto Plan enforced by the Paris Club—on the basis of the Toronto agreements of the G-7, which ended in Berlin at the 1981 annual reunion of the FMI World Bank—concerning the refunding of the debts of the LDCs to the rich countries is insufficient. This program addresses governments of rich countries about the severely indebted poorest nations, excluding the average-income and the low-income countries even if seriously indebted.

Concessionary debts owed to states, as bilateral debts owed to official institutions, do not undergo any restructuring.

Some creditor governments finance this restructuring with the funds meant for aiding development, thus reducing the commitment of Toronto.

Much more needs to be done in this direction, along the lines of what the Brady Plan requires from the banks, here too keeping in mind that the governments of the rich countries have special ethical and political responsiblities towards the poor countries.

## VI

Among the various elements to keep in mind, I believe the following points are particularly worthy of attention:

1. The problem of pulling certain highly indebted countries and regions out of the crisis is a systematic one which must be handled in a systematic manner, involving all creditors—not only the banks, but also governments and multilateral organizations, as well as all the institutions offering new loans.

2. The Brady Plan must be reinforced by means of major resources and coordinated management, possibly through an agency within the International Financial Institutions (IMF), and by also counting on the regional banks concerned with each "large area."

3. Following the example of the decisions of Toronto (option A) and Paris, there is the need for another reduction on the burden, different according to the level of development and indebtedness of the various categories of LDCs. Such a cut is obtained through the redistribution of the debt on a long term (thirty or forty years) and by applying interest taxes on different levels, according to the category of the countries.

4. For the poorest countries (group "IDA" only), an annulment of the debt service is imperative, as regards their past loans.

5. At any rate, in order to reinforce cuts on bilateral debts, payment conversions for interests in offset funds in local value are advisable to finance projects for development and environmental protection (such as the protection of tropical and equatorial forests, the development of human capital).

6. It is necessary to take into consideration a new "intermediate classification" not only to adjust and offer Toronto-type concessionary measures, to establish a redistribution of payments at reduced interest rates, as indicated in the fourth point, but also to carry out multilateral concessionary financing transactions.

7. An adequate flow of public and private resources must be guaranteed for the LDCs, thus creating all the necessary conditions for future development. This is why it is important to stress the target of 0.7

percent of the GNP for public aid to development on the part of the industrialized countries. Moreover, this figure was reconfirmed by the Ministerial Council of the DAC on May 14, 1990.

8. The various approaches to the different types of debts must be analyzed carefully: credits for aid; credits with a public guarantee; International Financial Institutions' loans; private loans. The debtor countries must receive certain privileges on the payments they owe to international institutions, through more solid concessionary means.

9. The LDCs—including the Eastern European countries—must decide on strict internal policies in agreement with the IFI. These arrangements must remain of a selective nature, tending to favour growth and more particularly protect the poorest social classes.

10. It is necessary to come out with—through appropriate incentives and well-organized work—more efficient support from banks in terms of the reductions needed on private debts' interest rates; fiscal and accounting laws should undergo some modifications in the industrialized countries, so as to favour the loaning banks working on reductions and new financing.

11. There is a possibility which should be investigated: that of President Mitterand, who suggested increasing the International Financial Institutions' concessionary resources, and granting the industrialized countries special drawing rights, which they can use to raise funds that will be used in the Brady Plan transactions; the rich countries will be favoured, and the interests will be reduced.

12. In many indebted countries endowed with an industrial structure or abounding in natural resources, it would be wise to push "swap" transactions further, with the establishment of mixed companies and the participation of foreign capital in privatized state companies, as well as BTO (build transfer operate) transactions and treasury bonds, providing these transactions with a public guarantee.

13. A special effort for East European countries should be made, giving them financial support in their transition period and allowing a fast change towards market economies, without creating serious social disruption.

14. To limit the past debt, it is necessary to substitute the debt reimbursement of the Eastern countries with the possibility for rich countries to participate in privatized enterprises ("debt-equity swap"), by establishing mixed companies and under the innovative conditions

we mentioned above. In the context of an "unbureaucratization" of such economic systems, it is necessary that the "new incoming money" policies substitute the offer of public debt with that of private debt.

15. In order to favour development plans, special attention should be given to the establishment and reinforcement of regional banks, like the European Bank for Reconstruction and Development launched by the EEC.

We have also suggested considering a bank for development for the Mediterranean (like the Japanese Overseas Finance Corporation and the Saudi Arabian Bank for Development), which will enable a growth of resources available in the area, the "relaunching" of coastal countries, as well as a solution to serious problems like the demographical increase and the emigration trends.

Drug trafficking, emigration from countries burdened with a drastic debt and unable to grow, the risk of environmental degradation, the instability of trade and the consequent impossibility of liberalizing it, and political instability are intensified by an unsettled and paralyzing debt problem, which can't be controlled without a well-developed economic system.

For the industrialized nations, the Third World's debt is a problem of common responsibility and security, which requires strong and determined commitment.

The UN expresses its clear position in favour of this great commitment.

# World Conference on the Less Poor Countries
## Paris, 4 September 1990

Four big problems, all intertwined, disturb the equilibrium and prosperity of our planet: wars, poverty, debt, and the environmental issue.

Throughout the entire decade of the eighties, Africa, Asia, the Middle East, and Latin America have all been tormented by guerrilla warfares between states and people, and groups which differed in their ideologies. Wars and guerrillas that caused destructions, indispensable migrations, persecutions, poverty. The level of the foreign debt, which oppresses so many low-income countries, is in part the consequence of armaments purchases and of military expenses, both necessary in those bloody wars and in fighting against permanent conditions of insecurity. However, oil's cost increase of the seventies and decrease of the eighties are also to blame. On one side, the oil-exporting countries, which represent a significant but not predominant share of the economic system of the developing countries—only 25 percent of the low-income economy and 12 percent of the average-income economy—have been running up debts. On the other side, the price increase of oil has created great difficulty for the economic systems of the developing countries importing oil (and most of them do). This is the reason these countries have had to resort to indebtedness abroad, something made very easy by the banks' intense commitment and their urge to recycle their large quantities of petrodollars. But the debt was bound to create problems. A debt which is impossible to pay generates further indebtedness. The African countries have caught themselves in a vicious cycle.

The debt has grown out of proportion, while in many developing countries poverty has worsened.

The cost of energy being very high and firewood still being the main resource of energy for the poor, more and more areas have become uninhabited. Urban poverty has generated environmental disasters.

Other elements such as drought, poor irrigation systems, and overuse of the pasture lands have contributed to this dramatic situation. Added to all this are the drawbacks of an abnormal demographic growth.

Out of the 5 billion people living on our planet, about 1 billion are defined poor in the World Bank's official statistics, excluding Taiwan.

This definition doesn't refer to approximate poverty or to a lack of welfare in rich countries, in which even the poor don't "die of hunger." It refers to absolute poverty; that is, to an availability of resources which is under that required for vital survival.

Statistics of poverty first take us to the south of Asia, where the poor are 500 million. Then Eastern Asia comes second, with its 280 million. Then follows sub-Saharan Africa, with its 180 million poor, holding the painful record of "very" poor. Half of the 360 million people living on this deserted side of the continent are in the poverty conditions known in Asia. But 36 percent have less than $200 per capita, versus 32 percent in Asia. In Latin America and the Caribbean, the poor—in the real sense of the word—are estimated to be 80 million. That is 22 percent of the 260 million population.

Another 80 million poor people live in the Middle East, in northern Africa, and in some parts of Europe.

It is known that in the eighties, the global situation of the poor improved, that their lifestyles and their life expectancy went slightly up.

Nevertheless, given a population growth of 2 percent in the Asian developing countries, 3 percent in Latin America and 3.2 percent in sub-Saharan Africa, the number of poor has definitely gone up, even if the percentage of poverty of the total population has gone down slightly. These are difficult statistics, and big figures hide some disastrous data, which is difficult to overlook.

This year, the statistics concerning the low-income countries—referring to the 1988 period—start with Mozambique, where earnings amount to $100 per inhabitant, followed by Ethiopia where an inhabitant's earnings reach $130, while Mozambique had $180 per capita.

Possibly, poverty hasn't expanded, but it certainly has become more intense.

In the speeches I gave in Geneva in the last few weeks, about the debt and development, I mentioned the example of the permanent income inequalities between Ethiopia with its $130 per capita and Switzerland with its $21,300 income: 160 times as much. A development expert pointed out that Ethiopia was in state of civil war. And in fact, it is not a question of an economic disaster due to a lack of resources or to the weight of the debt, but it is rather a question of political tragedy.

This is true for Ethiopia as well as for Mozambique and Sudan, Sri Lanka, Somalia, and other countries in Africa and other continents. This leads to two fundamental considerations. We must develop cooperation with these countries, so as to put an end to the local conflicts and reach peace, through new federal and confederal constitutional regulations and regional autonomy, as well as regional development projects, and then correctly support this initiative. It is our duty to reduce the debt and help primarily those countries which have followed the principle of respect for human rights and peace, and which now have to face reconstruction. It is imperative to concentrate political and financial efforts to break the perverse war-poverty tragedy. Naturally, other wars have to be avoided. Everything reasonable, possible and rightful must be done to avoid a conflict in the Gulf area, a conflict that would trigger a countless amount of destruction and tragic aftereffects.

An economist from the Brookings Institute stated that in a number of Latin American countries, because of the adjustment procedures required by the International Monetary authorities to come out of the debt crisis, the level of poverty went up 20 percent. This arouses complex and basic questions of selectivity and priority in the debt-poverty issue. In the adjustment plans suggested by the International Monetary Fund to the countries which because of high foreign debt have great difficulty in the balance of payments, a strong emphasis is placed on the reduction of food supplies and the increase in prices for oil and gas intended for commercial and household use. Certainly, it is necessary to prevent support from the public financing structure (and the public deficit) going to those who can do without it. However, selective steps can be taken. All this is true also because of the cost of energy, which in the domestic balance of the poor can have a dramatic repercussion.

Undernourishment is still a tough reality for one billion human beings. In India, almost 50 percent of the children up to five years of age are underfed, even after the gigantic efforts of that country to provide a minimum of nourishment to its entire population. In Bangladesh, a country afflicted by recurrent floods, the situation is even worse.

A quarter of the population of sub-Saharan Africa lives in a condition of chronic nourishment scarcity. The World Bank's suggested goal of an annual 4 percent growth of food production in this poor region involves a 2 percent increase of aid transfer of the GNP of the rich countries. A figure that is totally insignificant for wealthy countries: $4 billion annually on $15,000 million total income of these countries. But in this "hunger accounting," a strategy involving significant cuts of the debt reimbursement and public support for the new financing flows plays a predominant role.

In my opinion, the situation is so tragic in the poor countries that at least 90 percent of the reimbursement of the bilateral debt should be cancelled, while the other 10 percent would be converted into local currency and go to projects of economic development, human capital development, and environmental protection.

Similar measures should be thought of, in a smaller percentage, for the so-called intermediary countries. Besides, the DAC (committee of the representatives of the countries donating help to development), established within the OECD, stated a number of times that actual help given to development needs to be doubled, increasing it to 0.70 percent of the GNP of the industrialized countries, from the actual 0.35 percent, and this would mean $50 billion more per year.

The proposal of cancelling, whether totally or partially, the debt service owed to governments or their institutions would cost annually 0.10 percent of the GNP. To this should be added—as soon as possible—at least an identical percentage of new aid, primarily meant to fight poverty and spur investments for development in the countries which have been working with commitment in the mentioned areas.

It can be demonstrated that a peaceful context and intensified aid to development will help the poorest countries achieve solid growth. This will then enable them to overcome starvation before the year 2020, in spite of the population growth phenomenon which should anyhow be limited through persuasive family-planning campaigns.

A report on the debt presented to the UN at the Houston Summit of the world and government leaders is available for examination. The Houston Summit did adopt the proposal of extending the existing measures to obtain a systematic annulment of the debt for governments of the poorest countries. It also did adopt another of my suggestions: that of establishing measures to carry out Toronto-style reductions on the debt for governments of the semipoor countries too, that is the so-called intermediate countries (those between $500 and $1,200 per capita).

But in this framework of mind, it is necessary to limit cost increases on oil prices, avoiding situations similar to the one now witnessed on the spot markets.

Poor countries usually buy spot oil, because they don't have financial means and because they don't have any room for depositing. The poor importing countries are the first to be seriously afflicted by an oil crisis and by the price increases of oil.

The transfer of resources from poor countries which import oil to the oil-producing countries is becoming more and more unbearable. After the recent events, two important topics have reemerged strongly: that of peace in full respect of human rights and that of energy to be provided at a reasonable cost. Both are important topics that interest not only and mainly advanced industrialized countries, their well-being and their internal peace, but particularly the poor countries, their development, their fight against poverty and starvation in the world. Within a viewpoint of the world and of the international community, peace and development are more and more perceived as prospects and values that go hand in hand.

# Getting Out of the Debt Crisis Back on the Path of Development
# UNO General Assembly
# New York, 23 October 1990

My general report offers various proposals and suggestions on the different types of loans, the different kinds of poor, semipoor and so-called average-income countries, and the various regional areas.

Debts to banks, governments and governmental institutions, and multilateral financial organizations (IFI) imply different problems, with different responsibilities. But the crisis being a systematic one, the only efficient, long-lasting solution to these problems is an action involving all the components of the system.

Of all long-term debts, debts to private institutions now only amount to half: $465 billion in 1989, versus $466 to official creditors. Among these, the IFI have loaned $200 billion.

Therefore, there is principally a responsibility and commitment on behalf of governments, directly and indirectly, with respect to official loans.

First of all, it is suggested to cancel entirely the bilateral loans' service for the poor countries. Ninety percent of the service should be removed by attributing it to the national budgets, so as to dilute the cost for the loaning states' budgets. The remaining 10 percent would be transformed in long-term loans, at IDA (2 percent rate, thirty or forty years accrual) conditions and paid in indexed local currency. The residual sum should go to counterpart funds, also built up through the contributions of the indebted governments, international organizations and nonprofit organizations, for purposes of economic development, environment and human capital defense and use, infancy protection, drug and drug-traffic eradication.

For the intermediate-income countries—that is the ones earning between $500 and $1,200 per inhabitant—the same type of procedure is needed, with percentages of annulment of the bilateral debt service arranged between 60 percent and 80 percent.

Reductions should be inferior—while the technical procedure remains identical—for bilateral creditors, when it comes to the so-called average-income countries. (Allocations to counterpart funds should also be regulated according to the countries' income levels.)

On the whole, the loaning countries' burden for national budgets should not go beyond 0.1 percent of the GNP of the industrialized countries.

As for credit coming from the IFI, I think that more facilities should be granted and that the actual restrictions should be extended to the average-income countries; the possibility of granting again particular facilities to those countries afflicted by a special crisis (like energy) should be carefully examined. It is necessary to give the IFI a new and more dynamic role again, in the procedures of reconversion adjustments, of infrastructures development, and financial support to the Brady Plan. Of course, this involves granting the IFI adequate means, something possible by using special withdrawing rights which are made available through the resolution of increasing the shares of the International Monetary Fund.

Concerning banks' credits, the Brady Plan represents a courageous step in the right direction. However, it should be reinforced, starting by making more funds available, so as to reach the largest amount of countries possible, big and small simultaneously, in various continents, at a greater speed than the one used until now; but also to increase the efficiency, adapting it to the paying capacity of the indebted countries.

These measures should be kept in mind while also taking into consideration the relation between the interest rate which remains at their expense after the reconversion and the growth rate of the gross product: for this, discounts are necessary on capitals and on interests, and they should be slightly superior to the 30–35 percent ones which were until now applied; the tendency should range between 50 percent and 60 percent. But in order to accomplish our goal, it is important to increase guarantees on residual credits, according to the debt service and to its amount. This involves the availability of greater funds for the financing of the plan, as well as a fiscal regime of banking and accounting controls which will facilitate these transactions.

There should be other reinforcement measures for the Brady Plan, with regard to the bridge financings. This would allow the speeding up of transactions and the incentives of the banks which are ready to join in within a short period of time, providing adequate deterrents for those banks trying to attribute restructuring costs to ther creditors. For those countries with a very low-paying capacity, mostly because their per-capita income is low or low to average—when their debt has a low value on the secondary market—it will be necessary to set up the necessary financial means to effect major redemptions of this debt. All this must be done in the framework of domestic and international policies geared to recover the solvency and the credit worthiness of these states.

In the course of my visits to major banking institutions of the world in Europe, the U.S.A. and Japan, I have encountered—even if with different emphasis in each—a positive and concrete interest in assisting developing countries. This interest must be stimulated and strengthened through a series of measures, so as to reactivate the transfer of capital from the developed countries to the developing countries. In the private area, this transaction had dangerously started to disappear in the last decade. These measures include prioritarily cofinancing, insurance warranties, and coinsurance on behalf of multilateral and bilateral public financing organizations.

Besides, the forms of new finance must be diversified to avoid repeating any of the past errors.

Latin America and the Caribbean have immense resources, which were not properly exploited due to the debt-service burden. In the eighties, the aggregate gross product went up only 1 percent annually, and as a consequence the per-capita income only went up 0.1 percent annually: only 10 percent in that decade.

The lack of growth affected the paying capacity. The crisis got worse and worse.

In my opinion, for Latin America and the Caribbean, a reduction and recycling plan should be set, so as to clear and subsequently reverse, thanks to public and private contributions, the current annual $25 billion financial downflow.

In the first place, for bilateral official credits, governments should carry out reductions and cuts similar to those accepted as necessary by commercial banks, in the Brady Plan.

The IFIs have a balance between donations and payments with Latin America which, at the moment, amounts to zero. It is necessary for it to turn positive, through special means similar to those adopted for the poorest countries.

The third important point concerns development aid in order to finance the infrastructures, boost the "new incoming money" initiatives of the market forces, in the production and the diversification of exports.

Another very important point is the financing and strengthening of the Brady Plan.

There is a need for firmer, more solid incentives when it comes to greater reductions of interests, and to the debts' amount. In this frame of mind, it is also necessary to examine the possibility for certain countries, for a share of the interests to be deposited in indexed local currency warrants, which are convertible at par situated locally.

Highy transferable financial means of repayment are needed for redemption operations, which in certain cases simply seem the best solution, and which in others should be viewed as one of the many available choices.

In Asia, the debt problem stands out in the southern part—which includes India principally, Pakistan, and Sri Lanka.

This part of the Asian continent—which has a GNP of $345 billion—has 30 percent (1989) of the world population and half of the world's poor (46.4 percent in 1985). Its per-capita income amounts to $280.

South Asia's GNP growth rate in the 1980–89 period was 5.5 percent, while the 1989 decline (4.8 percent) still is proof of a development rate which stands among the highest in the large areas of the world.

However, according to the World Bank, in the year 2000, there will still be 350 million poor people in South Asia.

This shows how the debt which still burdens some of these countries is—in any case—a problem which needs constant attention.

Development in South Asia must be based on two pillars: an increase of agriculture adapted to the population increase, and an increase of the differential industrial sector to change the productive structure and modernize it.

The World Bank, in its report on poverty, writes that "progress in Asia depends on development in China and India. If the economic reforms fail in China, if India is incapable of keeping its recent rhythm, attempts in lowering the poverty rates will be quite less successful."

These two countries receiving so little financial support for their development need the IDA type of aid for infrastructures and investments.

Bangladesh, a country of 110 million inhabitants, shares the record for poverty with sub-Saharan Africa: Its per-capita GDP amounts to $170 in 1988; and in the early eighties half the population lived in extreme poverty, in the complete incapacity of obtaining enough food to live "a reasonably active life."

Bangladesh must come first in being relieved from the debt service owed to governments.

Up until now, Pakistan has been able to face up to its obligations of servicing the debt, thanks to its favorable deadlines, but the growth of the financing of the public deficit by means of foreign debt can make the situation much worse.

The debt of sub-Saharan Africa now amounts to $145 billion.

In sub-Saharan Africa, in the 1980–86 period, under the encumbrance of these debts, the gross product went down 3.1 percent per inhabitant, while consumptions underwent a 2.4 percent fall and exports were reduced 2.1 percent annually in real terms, thus worsening the relation between the debt service and exports.

Because of the worsening of the terms of trade (by 13 percent), imports went down even more: 7.5 percent annually, while simultaneously reducing new investments, upkeeping and consumptions.

The overall flow of resources, thanks to the multilateral and bilateral loans, makes up 7.3 percent of the GNP, of which the sum assigned to investment is only 2.3 percent. The consequence is a worrying decline of the capital accumulation from 21 percent to 17.5 percent between the beginning and the end of the eighties.

We might say that the economic problem of the sub-Saharan countries, without drastic cuts to their debt and without exceptional concessionary measures from the IMF or World Bank, seems unresolvable.

Even though my general report was finished little before the Gulf crisis, after the Iraqi invasion of Kuwait, the North African and Middle East regions do receive the special attention they deserve in this report.

This is because it is a matter of a specific area of interdependence between creditors and debtors. It is so particularly in the case of the EEC countries with Mediterranean interests and the rich countries of the Gulf which produce oil on one side, and the indebted Afro-Arabic countries of this region on the other side.

Between 60–70 percent of most of these countries' debt is to their government and governmental institutions. I believe it necessary to suggest first of all a moratorium and special reconversion interventions, as well as aid financing on behalf of such financing organizations, in order to protect the fragile equilibriums from the actual crisis and to launch economic recovery procedures.

Likewise, in this framework it is necessary for the donating Arab countries to make an extra effort and unite their work with that of the OECD's multilateral and bilateral action. Certainly, the exceptional critical situation discloses new problems and introduces negative factors which force the reexamination of the entire situation.

At the end of 1988, the East European debt (USSR excluded) amounted to $100 billion, of which 40 percent was for Poland's and 20 percent for Hungary's.

The debt is often the result of the inefficiency of the collectivistic enterprises whose governments worried about settling their deficits and financed themselves through foreign loans or at the expense of the population.

After the collapse of the Communist regimes, great progress was achieved in terms of market economies in Poland and Hungary. Czechoslovakia is undergoing courageous changes in price planning, in organizing capital, services, and employment; and, thanks to a reinforcement of public financings, similar experiments are being carried out in other countries.

The strategies used in these countries for recovering from the debt and the availability of new incoming money must assure us that old mistakes will not be repeated or that other similar ones will not be made. These strategies must favor the rapid transition process, through financings at the enterprise level. The public debt must be substituted with private debt and direct investment, and with innovative new finance formulas, based on the projects and on the exploitation of raw materials and international commercial collaboration.

It is important to explore the possibility of constituting a payments union for the European East, with financial assistance from the EEC, as was done with Western Europe after the Second World War.

Establishing free trade areas associated with the EEC, in conformance with the political lines of large regional areas, can be in this context much more efficient than large granted loans from governments to governments.

In the last decade, the sum granted by the donating countries to the developing countries fluctuated around $45 billion, according to the 1987 purchasing power. It went up as far as $50 billion in 1985, then it dropped slowly, getting near to the levels of the beginning of the decade. Finally, it rose back to $50 billion, at par with the same percentage of the 1980 GNP, but last year there was another drop, which is now worrying us all.

It is necessary to double development aid, taking it to the 0.70 percent of the GNP of the donating countries. Such a percentage, according to the calculations made in the various decades and gradually reconfirmed by the DAC, is the necessary amount to enable development aid to reach an acceptable level for growth.

In fact, an additional $60 billion entirely devoted to development, with a ratio of capital to income of four and a multiplier of two for the attraction of private financing, could generate $30 billion of added gross product per year, equal to 1 percent of the GNP of the developing countries. This would raise the growth rate of the per-capita income from the average 3 percent of the last two decades to 4 percent, versus an average growth of our 2.0–2.5 percent per-capita product.

All this is rightful and necessary. It is also rightful and necessary that the debtor states commit sincerely to doing their share.

First of all, these countries must become aware of how to reorganize their own public finances, how to increase fiscal pressure and avoid the necessary and just social and economic incentives to be wasted in some kind of assistance which is not justified.

"Pharaonic" projects are to be avoided and profitability should be calculated with more care. The public enterprises should be managed as limited companies with their own balances, and where the public economy is too expanded, they should be privatized entirely or partly so as to work towards a market economy's increasing space for local entrepreneurship and joint ventures.

Without any rules, economy, finance, and banking would be a dangerous adventure; but discriminating restrictionism and dirigism create a damaging bureaucratic conception, which curtails domestic savings, fosters indebtedness, and weakens development.

The irresponsible massive capital exportations on behalf of the citizens of the indebted countries is inadmissible, but it is also necessary to develop appropriate methods of savings, which will be protected from inflation in order to draw the developing capital to the domestic market, through the various transactions of tourism, immigrant remittances, and international trade.

Of course, this also includes fighting inflation by giving priority to the fiscal and income policy.

Some adjustments have to be settled, but they shouldn't repress investment and then have a harmful effect in the long run.

Accomplishing all this is difficult but not impossible, as is well shown by the experience of the countries which have managed to come out of the debt crisis or are gradually coming out, and which at the same time are developing democracy and freedom.

A significant leadership and a systematic action are the solution to the complex debt problems. Therefore, an agency or committee within the World Bank and International Monetary Fund is needed, with contributions from—for each of the large indebted areas, such as Mediterranean Africa and the Middle East, sub-Saharan Africa, Latin America, Asia, the European East—the regional development banks and from other multilateral organizations of regional dimension, whether already existing or to be created.

Furthermore, it should be more and more clear that the future of peace is linked to the prospect of new regional areas, based on cooperation between industrialized countries and developing countries and on the respect of the various peoples' rights and identities.

It is necessary to plan an institutional basis and rules for such regional corporations and some new significant forms of cooperation for the large areas in crisis, finally putting the most recent proposals into concrete action.

Economic development, peace, and respect of people's rights are three inseparable components of this project, on which I would like the international community to make a strong commitment.

# Statement Made by Craxi Rome, 26 October 1990

I wish to thank Prof. John Kenneth Galbraith for the invaluable support he has given to the thesis discussed in the debt-issue report which I've recently submitted to the United Nations General Assembly. I thank him for having rightfully acknowledged that one of the most pressing problems is the total annulment of the debt for the poorest countries. Some countries—including Italy and others—are already supporting this solution and, hopefully, others will follow the example.

Galbraith has justly underlined how aid to the developing countries and the connected debt problem represent one of the main targets and duties of our time, which requires major attention from the international community and the more advanced and industrialized countries.

Professor Galbraith has also made valuable suggestions on other actual and significant issues—like the need to prioritize the Third World countries and the transformation processes initiated in Eastern Europe—which, in my opinion, deserve full attention and support. These countries have seen their planned economies collapse and need our support—through credits and transfer of technology—for their purchase and consumption goods sector, so as to spur small enterprise. I do again agree with Professor Galbraith when he discusses the problems of compatibility between production and environmental protection and suggests setting or extending tax incentives for those starting up environmental clean-up processes. Regarding the economic consequences of the Gulf crisis, he points out the urge to focus on the poorest countries, which are facing drastic expenses, and to put a stop to all speculative manipulations through a resolute use of strategic resources. He concludes by stressing the need to reexamine alternative resources carefully, so as to reduce energy dependence, which in some countries is very intense; as we know, this is the case in Italy.

# Conference on Cooperation for Development
# Rome, 17 October 1991

Currently, policies of solidarity and developmental aid for the less favoured countries are placed in a very different international context.

From a political and military point of view, the world is no longer split into two opposed blocs. Reality has gone beyond national imagination. The goal of reducing the percentage of the gross national product devoted to military expenses on the part of the industrial countries appears to be near, or at least more within reach. The reconversion of at least part of the military strength expense into productive and domestic investments, to achieve economic and social development primarily in the less developed countries, is possible, in addition to being reasonable and fully justified.

A sharp reduction of the mandatory military service will surely contribute to savings on public expenses.

Of course, it is right to say that this procedure will necessarily be gradual, that a reconversion could require specific costs and that the economy of expenditures in the countries with international payment deficits should take place principally through a net reduction in the public debt. But this statement doesn't take into consideration the enormous diversity between the military expenditure percentages of the gross product and the expenditure for development aid. On average, the first one is about 5.4 percent in the Western industrial countries (just like in the developing countries), while it was as much as 11.5 percent in the USSR until not long ago. In the Eastern European countries, the official military expenditure was considered quite lower (about 3 percent), but the military industry, specializing in export, was very strongly developed. Instead, the percentage of development aid on the gross product of the industrial countries belonging to the OECD (that is, to the DAC: Development Aid Committee) is more than ten times inferior to that of the military expenditure.

In 1990, it was about 0.35 percent of the GNP, with a margin going from 0.21 percent for the U.S., to 0.27 percent for the United Kingdom, to 0.31 percent for Japan, 0.32 percent for Italy, 0.42 percent for Germany—and Canada and Belgium are close to this figure—while

France gave 0.55 percent, and Holland and the Scandinavian countries gave 1 percent.

On the whole, in 1990, the OECD countries gave $54 billion in development aid. Twenty-five billion of this sum came from states within the European Community.

Instead, the military expenses of the OECD countries in 1990 were about $700 billion and those of the states belonging to the European Community were about $200 billion.

All that would be needed is that a twentieth part of the military expenditure of the industrial countries—35 billion—be assigned to the development aid, and there would be an exceptional increase of the financial resources for international economic and social cooperation.

The new political context for peace makes the responsibilities of the Europeans, and of Westerners in general, greater and more pressing, compared to the economic and social problems of the rest of the world.

The multicoloured question of the conversion of the East European and Soviet economies is a prominent issue. It can't be solved without adequate financial support. It would be rather illusory to expect the public insurances to solve the problem by conferring direct aid, loans intended for aid and loans granted, in a reckless manner. Commercial and industrial initiatives can't turn into donations, and great responsibility must be kept toward economic collaboration and entrepreneurial initiatives.

The work of the G-7 in favor of the Soviet Union, however, still involves a complex negotiation, not only with the USSR, but also with the fifteen republics, at a moment of great institutional vagueness, political confusion and uncertainty. Besides, the emergencies that have sprung in the East—including the new migratory tendencies and the huge amount of unemployed, which has become the new spectre in the ex-Communist area—have in fact affected the already modest resources of aid coming from the industrial countries, reducing those available for cooperation with the "Third World" countries.

The solutions to the foreign debt problem of these countries, which are engaging themselves, on the basis of intiatives from the international organisms and governments, in a cooperation between creditors and debtors, could well be jeopardized by the request of financial resources for the East. That is why a global expansion policy of all available means for world cooperation is necessary.

For many of the Third World countries, the burden of the debt continues to be a great drawback for possible development, and a hindrance for the new international investment initiatives, which could be of interest not only for the south but also for the northern part of the world. Instead, the reductions (agreed on and adjusted according to each situation) of the debts towards governments, banks and international financing institutions, by stimulating and giving support to the necessary internal adjustment procedures of the indebted countries, constitute a very powerful element for the diffusion of the economic growth process.

We are talking about a development which is still based on a number of inequalities, especially if we consider the per-capita income instead of the total income. In 1992, the northern part of the world and Asia should be expected to witness a new growth of their economy. Even the Middle East shows a number of positive signs. However, Africa, Latin America, the USSR and some of Eastern Europe remain stagnant in terms of per-capita income.

It also must not be forgotten that poverty, starvation, personal and environmental degradation, and infectious diseases—from tuberculosis to AIDS—are present in the daily lives of more than 800 million people in Asia, Africa, and Latin America, while other cases of poverty start to give signs in the Central European area.

Therefore, an increase of resources for economic growth and humanitarian aid in all the cases mentioned are rightful, even if, very unfortunately, it is true that a part of these resources have been sometimes wasted or used in an improper manner. Just the same, no hypocritical justification based on wastes and inefficiencies can cancel the extremely negative fact that we are dangerously and unjustly diminishing our commitment to many of these countries, at a moment which is absolutely crucial for them.

The increase of expenditures on aid is not the only solution, however. A world financing strategy oriented towards expansion, such as the one that characterized the period after the Second World War, is also needed. This kind of a strategy requires an increase of the world monetary liquidity, through the new shares of the International Monetary fund and other policies contrived which would allow reductions of interest rates in the dollar, yen, and EMS monetary area.

Some documents of the important financing organisms have been, for some time, putting emphasis on the pecularity of the real interest rates of the eighties. These, at 4 percent and sometimes more, have been double, and at certain times more than double, the average long-term rates of our century.

Therefore, the reduction of the real interest rates corresponds to the opening of normalization of the cost of money, meant to give long-term investments greater and more natural profitability than those reductions from actual unnatural rates.

This reduction will also allow a reasonable relief to the public budgets of the countries indebted abroad or in their own territory, whose debt service is artificially raised by the high world rates.

Therefore, a straight "no" to a restrictive fiscal policy followed by a widening of liquidity; a big "yes" to simultaneous fiscal and monetary actions.

Here too, Europe must know how to play its role.

After having undergone a steady increase, on a GNP percentage, from 0.20 percent in the 1980–84 period, up to 0.40 percent in 1986, Italian aid to development went back to a fluctuating condition, going down to 0.35 percent in 1987, continuing to 0.39 percent in 1988, and readjusting to 0.42 percent in 1989. But ever since that year, our help to development has gone down drastically, as far as 0.32 percent of the gross national product in 1990. France's aid went up from 0.44 percent of the GNP in 1986, to 0.50 percent in 1989, and to 0.55 percent in 1990.

Germany has maintained its share of aid at about 0.40 percent of the GNP while Great Britain has now, for many years, been keeping at a modest but steady percentage of 0.27–0.30 percent of the GNP. In the presence of new needy countries in the East, the downward phase of the percentage of development aid on the gross product means that signed records, commitments, and projects already initiated in the Third World countries must be disregarded, reduced, or postponed without any certain date.

The laying of the financial law for 1992 makes the Italian role in the International Cooperation Policy less and less credible.

We are talking of a drastic cut of the allocation of the law in force, for what concerns the law 49 of 1987 and the law 173 for 1990 on financings for the developing countries.

The $820 billion figure for aid to development of the law 49 remains unchanged. After the $250 billion being added to this sum and set aside under a new heading for the Eastern European countries, the inclusive figure represents about 0.225 percent of the GNP of 1992. The surplus will help to reach 0.25 percent of the GNP, going back to the 1984 level!

In the face of this quantitative degradation in development aid, almost halved in a short time, we find in the 1992 financial budget an item of $1,800 billion for SACE's activities, in addition to the ordinary annual funding of $430 billion. And this with a statement saying that the special grant above mentioned would have to be "adjusted after close examination of the risks taken by the autonomous section, as far as the exporters are concerned, especially in the Middle Eastern area, which is afflicted by well-known war events."

This topic is a very touchy one. However, seen from this angle, it all seems like a particular political goal, which was discussed, agreed on, and described a number of times in front of Parliament, before being completely twisted around.

Seeing that all commitments with multilateral organizations represent a cost of more than $1,600 billion for 1992, while $250 are reserved to aid for the European Eastern countries, one will wonder how much is actually left for the Cooperation Fund.

Certainly, a true commitment must always exist between policies intended for aid, peace and respect of the basic human and economic rights in the countries being helped. There must be a link between infrastructural aid, emergency aid, social-welfare aid, and the financing of economic initiatives, for a serious financial commitment based on principles of a healthy market economy, on behalf of the countries assisted.

However, this is not possible if the overall commitment diminishes.

It would be a very serious moral and political error, at a moment when the need to rebuild peace everywhere is being expressed, if some country withdrew, instead of cooperating to the construction of a new and more balanced reality.

Italy will therefore assign 0.30 percent (0.35 percent with the surplus) of its gross product to cooperation and solidarity with the developing countries.

This appears to be the least that could be done. We are only talking about half of that 0.75 percent commitment which the OECD repeatedly stated as being necessary from the industrialized countries.

If helping with two hands is not possible yet, it is important to manage helping at least with one. But it has to be an entire hand.

# Development in Africa:
# A Commitment of Common Interest
# New York, 28 October 1991

African development continues to show two negative characteristics: a low per-capita income level and a growth rate of the gross product which, with some exceptions, does not seem to adapt to the high growth rate of the population and to the food requirements, while the environment is put to a severe test by the desperate fight for survival.

The industrialized world has significant responsibilities and great duties towards Africa for many historical reasons and even more recent ones, if we think of the colonial and the postcolonial period.

While, in the new scenery, the curtain drops on antagonism between the West and the Soviet bloc, Africa, no longer a highly strategic political-military scene, must not run the risk of being abandoned.

We often forget the past situation of this continent was partly the consequence of impositions or conditionings due to the quarrels between the two blocs.

I think, instead, that the search for common values should become much easier.

Certainly, new attention on Africa is needed from the rich people. This attention had become more intense in the mideighties, when the African continent found itself struck by drought and the desertification increased, together with famine and locust.

The years that followed certainly didn't solve the drastic problems which then arose in front of the very eyes of the high-income countries.

If we take sub-Saharan Africa into consideration, in terms of population and territory, figures are in a great measure worse than the ones gathered then. In the decade of the eighties, the per-capita product went down 1.2 percent per year. In 1989, the per-capita product amounted to $340. The total product amounted to $160 billion, for about half a billion people.

The 830 million inhabitants of the high-income countries have, in 1989, over $15 trillion: one hundred times the income of sub-Saharan Africa. In the last two decades, the gap has become even more obvious, because the per-capita product of sub-Saharan Africa has gone down another three points, while that of the high-income countries went up two and a half.

The half billion people living in sub-Saharan Africa have, on the whole—including all aid—an income equal to that of Switzerland. It has an immediate food deficit, which the United Nations' Organization for world food planning considers to be 2 million tons of equivalent grain.

Thirty million people, especially in Ethiopia, Sudan, Angola, Liberia, Mozambique, Nigeria, and Somalia, are about to die because of undernourishment.

Policies of food supply are hindered by the lack of infrastructures and distribution networks, on top of the destruction caused by civil wars. However, the main obstacle is the lack of financial resources, due to the balance-of-payments imbalance and to the drying out of currency reserves.

The last Report of the World Bank states that arable land went down from 0.5 hectares per person in 1965 to 0.3 in 1987. This represents a 40 percent decrease.

The sub-Saharan African problem of energy, which is linked to the shortage of currency, causes a continuous exacerbated type of pressure for the people of this territory. In fact, firewood supplies 80 percent of the energy needed by sub-Saharan Africa and its supply capacity is diminishing every day. As this resource diminishes, manure and harvest residues are more and more used as combustibles instead of as fertilizers. Overgrazing is intense. More than a quarter of the 750 million hectares are undergoing desertification; the agricultural potential there is very difficult to recuperate.

In the most recent ten years, the destruction of forests has affected 35,000 square kilometers per year: a surface equal to that of Italy and Holland put together.

Nevertheless, Africa has a hydroelectric potential of 300,000 megawatts, of which less than 4 percent is exploited. The situation is similar for oil and natural gas resources.

Among the tragedies of sub-Saharan Africa, there is also the development of AIDS. Out of the 10 million people affected by AIDS since 1985, 5.5 million are in Africa and the greatest part in sub-Saharan Africa. In some of the capitals of Central Africa—according to the World Bank's report of 1991—more than 50 percent of the people having entered hospitals are affected by this disease. This means less space (which was already limited) in the hospitals for other diseases and leads to a drain of funds, at the nations' health expense.

Surely, development aid amounts to a significant share of the gross product of sub-Saharan Africa: on average, 7.5 percent of their income. One might wonder how, in spite of this aid being given, the growth rate of the gross product of these countries is so low. There are various explanations for this problem, mostly related to the vicious cycle of poverty. This is what was found out from examining the trend of the gross product for consumptions and investments of these countries in the last few years. In 1980, investments amounted to $45 billion out of $225 billion income, equal to 20 percent of the overall income. In 1986, the income of this region had gone down to $168 billion. Investment had gone back up $1 billion; therefore, its percentage of the GNP was around 15 percent. An exceptional effort, when one considers that the total consumption, in one year, had dropped from $172 to $148 billion, while the population had increased 3.5 percent. But the drop in prices of the raw materials had caused a decline in exportations, which had led (together with the problems of economy and public finance) to interrupting and reducing the debt service drastically.

There was an ensuing slow and hesitant increase which in 1990 is equal to $190 billion, obviously including aid, while the thin exports managed to pull even with imports. Moreover, investments only amount to $28 billion, which is equal to 15.5 percent of the entire income.

Of course, this being a very modest figure, one cannot expect the growth rate of the gross product to be much more.

As a consequence, low income leads to a limited saving capacity and to a modest availability of the resources for private and public investments. This obstructs a high development of the product and makes way to limited fiscal bases, perpetuating a lack of infrastructures and upkeeping, which are—together with the drastic restraint in professional training—among the most significant causes for a reduced productivity and for the difficulty of diversifying productions and exportations. Then, the burden of the debt is on top of that.

In these conditions, most of that seven percent of the income, formed with the development aid, is used to keep the level of survival and economic subsistence which would otherwise collapse. The World Bank foresees a 0.5 percent growth of the per-capita product by the year 2000 for sub-Saharan Africa: a positive hypothesis, compared to the frightening decline of the eighties, but this surely isn't enough to solve the problems of poverty or supply the needed resources to launch virtuous development.

In Mediterranean Africa, we find different situations, in terms of income levels, regarding the population increase.

The economies of Algeria and Libya have a per-capita product of $2,300 and $5,600 with 24 million inhabitants, and 4 million inhabitants, respectively. Tunisia, with its 8 million inhabitants, has a $1,230 per-capita income. Egypt, a country which was strongly struck by the area's crisis in multiple aspects of its economy—from tourism to trade on the Suez Canal to the immigrant remittances—has an income which is slightly above $500 per capita (and according to some figures, below). Egypt having 50 million inhabitants and Morocco having 24 million, we can say that two-thirds of the population of Northern Africa has a low-average or low income. Therefore, the debt burden continues to be a problem which should be considered with constant attention.

All these countries share one big issue: the scarcity of the actually cultivable territory with respect to the population whose growth rate is significant and fraught with consequences for all the Mediterranean states and, consequently, for the entire European continent. The present population growth rate is around 2.5 percent in Egypt and Tunisia, around 2.7 percent in Morocco, over 3 percent in Algeria, and 4 percent in Libya.

According to the demographical expectations, therefore, Mediterranean Africa is doomed to jump from the current 110 million inhabitants to 150 million by the end of this century and reach 229 million in 2025.

On one hand, inhabitants of the European countries of the EEC in the Mediterranean are now 172 million. They are expected to become, without taking into consideration other eventual immigrations, 182 million in 2025. Presently, they have 60 million more inhabitants than Mediterranean Africa, and in a little more than thirty years, that is a generation, they will be 50 million more than in North Africa. And that is without taking into account the 50 million inhabitants of Turkey, which in the year 2025 will have gone up to 90 million, and without taking into consideration that in 2025 the sub-Saharan African population will probably account for 160 million Ethiopians, 300 million Nigerians, 110 million Kenyans and Ugandans, 140 million Tanzanians and Zairians, 60 million Sudanese, and so on.

On the other hand, the difference in per-capita income between the two shores of the Mediterranean is extremely high: about ten times.

Surely, with a tendency similar to the hydraulic principle of the communicating vessels, the migrating wave would be enormous.

Therefore, the issue of mutual dependence between Europe and North Africa is evident. Development and economic cooperation, cultural and institutional cooperation must be intensified between the two areas, so as to defuse the demographic bomb and so as to promote a balanced relationship between resources and population, exploiting as well as possible the local and regional resources, so that emigration doesn't reach overwhelming levels.

This makes far-reaching and urgent relaunching strategic steps absolutely necessary in Africa.

This procedure should begin with at least a tenth immediately; gradually, another tenth of the military expenses of the Western countries, which amount to 5.5 percent of their gross product (therefore about $800 billion), must be earmarked, in various ways, for additional investments for the less developed countries and for the East European countries. This is the only way to loosen the pressure on the resource requirements and help investment in the countries of the Soviet bloc and work towards recovery in the Middle East. According to International Monetary Fund estimates, such requirements amount to about $100 billion annually in the next five years. Such pressure, if not counterbalanced, is doomed to having a very negative impact on the availability of financial means, for ordinary investments, aid credits, and aid to the Third World's countries.

It also appears imperative to carry out the rate increase of the International Monetary Fund and the expanding of liquidity which can support a lasting reduction of interest rates, in a context of widespread economic growth and of trade development.

For a decade now, the prevailing average real interest rate in the world has been 4 percent; in the developing countries, it is 6 percent and double of that registered in the history of world economics. This is unnatural and makes the solution to the debt problem artificial, braking investment, reducing the space public finance should have for the infrastructural policies and for the long-term exploitation of natural resources.

Considering the particular case of Africa, the first strategic thought is that West Europe has special commitments and responsibilities, because of its tight interdependence with the African continent. But it is important that each do its share, given that some problems and lines of intervention—such as the liberalization of trade—regard every single rich country.

In my opinion, these are the actions we must carry out in Africa:

1. Continuing, amplifying, and speeding up the remission of official credit to poor and semi-poor countries, especially those in urgent conditions.
2. Carrying on and increasing actions by the International Financial Institutions (IFI) geared to supplying the indebted poor and semipoor countries with the grant of special very long-term loans, at very favourable conditions.
3. Continuing and improving the modifications and reductions of official credits made by the Club di Parigi, extending—at set conditions—the concessions also to the periods following the ones mentioned in the previous agreements.
4. Extending and reinforcing the Brady Plan, in terms of bank credits for the average-income African countries in the framework of coordinated intervention programs which will also include the amounts from governments and from the IFI.
5. Developing swap interventions of debts to governments, to enterprises and corporations assisted by public insurances, in funds for the environment which will also be financed through other means. Protecting forests, recuperating desertified land, and safeguarding and cleaning the sea should all be at the top of the list.
6. Developing coordinated sanitary interventions geared—in particular—to fight the more infectious diseases such as AIDS.
7. Developing bilateral and multilateral interventions for professional training, and for inserting, with flexible conditions, the actual or eventual emigrants in the European work market.
8. Favoring the development of investments and collaboration in the African economic initiatives of the industrialized

enterprises' countries, through suitable liberalization processes and through local laws based on a general respect of rights to property and enterprises that will be standardized as much as possible.
9. Promoting infrastructures and agreements which will render possible the effective development of large unified African market areas, so as to permit new economic and commercial opportunities in large areas of regional demand.
10. Promoting and reinforcing financial and commercial agreements in which, for the service of long and average term loans made available by the bank system to the developing countries, future profits from contracts on supplies of their resources are used and guaranteed with fitting clauses which ensure the effective permanence and duration.
11. Generally speaking, innovative finance formulas and simplifications for the financing procedures of the joint ventures and of mixed companies, also allowing that the contracts be made not only within the ministries of the countries giving the aid credits, but also within bank institutions.

The socioeconomic and environmental progress of Africa is a common point of interest—and therefore, must be a common responsibility—of the African countries and of the industrialized nations, Europe particularly.

We have a common interest in safeguarding the seas and forests of Africa. We have a common interest in the use of African mineral, hydro, agricultural, and fishing resources and in protecting such environmental estate. It is our common interest to stop desertification, because climates are interdependent, and the red sands of the Sahara are already colouring the Alpine peaks.

It is in our common interest to make use of the human capital of Africa, in a balanced relationship between geographical areas and cultures. It is in our common interest to secure peace and submit the expenditures meant for armaments and war to purposes of progress, justice, and human civilization.

# European Parliament Seminar: The Role of the UN in Promoting Development in the World
# Rome, 28 May 1992

According to some, the United Nations, as an institution, should not play a predominant role in the promotion of world economic and social development.

However, the preamble of the United Nations' Constitutional Charter clearly outlines the following goals: mutual tolerance between people and social aggregations; peace and security between nations; and use of the international economic assets to achieve economic and social progress in the interest of all civilizations.

The first article of the United Nations' Charter emphasizes international cooperation for economic, social, cultural development and human rights purposes. Article 13 states that carrying out research work and expressing recommendations for promoting international economic and social cooperation is part of the fundamental duties of the General Assembly of the UN. The Economic and Social Council transmits the outcome of this work to specialized agencies which work as reference points for the World Bank, FAO, UNICEF, UNDP, ILO, and the new UNCED, which is organizing this year the first World Conference on Environment and Development, in Rio de Janeiro.

According to article 56 of the treaty, each single member state is to cooperate with the UNO to achieve the peace and development aims mentioned in article 55.

That is a rule which is, as we all know, far from being respected. Because of the rich countries' behavior, financial obstacles stand in the way of an efficient carrying out of the United Nations' recommendations. This is the reality, even if these recommendations—as in the case of the Debt and Development Report—are approved at the summits of most of the industrialized countries and are well accepted by international public opinion and by high moral entities such as the Holy See.

We all know that the reluctance of some important governments to pay out their annual shares places the FAO in an extremely critical situation. We all know how important agricultural development is, especially for the Southern countries of the world, but also for the changing Eastern countries which are going through a terrible crisis.

But a true "green revolution" can only take place if technical assistance and investments are guaranteed, if the FAO's role becomes more significant and if the rich countries agree to take on a larger financial commitment.

Ever since it was created, the United Nations has found itself practically entirely absorbed by the very difficult upkeeping of the political balance and of security between the great opposed blocs.

Finally, walls, myths, and empires have collapsed. Since they are no longer tormented by those strategic responsibilities, the United Nations should now be able to work towards strengthening peace and human rights, concentrating on economic and social development, and on international economic, cultural, and environmental cooperation.

The "Security Council" should change into a "Security and Development Council" and turn to the great issues of interest of what remains of this century and of the next: the right of everyone to survival and to the minimum supplies granting a dignified human life; the reorganization of the states in the context of a new equilibrium and of new regional regulations; the relaunching of economic development and of international exchanges; and protection of all environmental and planetary resources.

Article 53 provides for the possibility of establishing organizations or regional agencies that would enforce the Security Council's regulations.

The report published last year by the UNDP on "human development" provides, through its theory on the great privatizations and differences between the rich and the poor, a picture of worries together with hopes, which the International Community should consider an ideal ground for reflection.

A year ago, there were still 800 million people starving in the world. This year, this figure went up because of the disintegrations and the conflicts that broke out after the collapse of the Soviet monolith.

About 900 million adults—in the developing countries—are still completely illiterate and 1.5 billion have no basic health assistance.

While 1.750 billion men, women, and children live without drinking water, more than 1 billion are in conditions of absolute poverty.

The average income per inhabitant in the south of the world is a twentieth of that in the north. And we are only talking about an average: One one side, Ethiopia and Mozambique have $100 per capita; on the other side, Switzerland has $30,000, which is 300 times as much. Italy has $15,000, which is 150 times as much. Asia has, on one side, Japan, with its $24,000 per inhabitant, and on the other side, India and China (2 billion people), earning a seventieth of that, with $350 per inhabitant. The maternal death rate in the south of the world is fifteen times that of the north; there are twelve times more children dying in their first five years of life in the south. Illiterate women account for 50 percent, and the total of illiterate adults account for 60 percent more than in the north.

Figures for life expectancy are quite different from one country to another in the south of the world. In most of sub-Saharan Africa, life expectancy ranges between forty-two and forty-six years of age, while in China it is seventy and in India and Pakistan it is fifty-eight to fifty-nine years of age.

The differences among these figures are dramatically astonishing, even if great progress has been achieved.

Development aid, even if thin still (at present 0.35 percent of the rich countries' product), has helped to diminish social gaps. The efforts and warnings made by the international organizations have not been in vain, and figures speak for themselves.

The report prepared on human development states that life expectancy, which, in the poor countries, is now fifty years of age, was a little below forty years of age thirty years ago.

While life expectancy in the rich countries went up from seventy to seventy-seven years of age, in the poor countries it went up 25 percent, and in the whole of the developing countries it went up 40 percent, from forty-five to sixty-two years of age. Certainly, this has caused a ratio diminution between the aggregate national product and the product per inhabitant, but it is the greatest of all victories for humanity, if life truly is a treasure.

Children's mortality in the south of the world has also shown a positive trend: in the poorest countries, it went from 17 percent to 12.5 percent, and overall in the developing countries it went from 15 percent to 8 percent.

Literacy has gone up from 30 to 40 percent for adults in the poorest countries, and from 42 percent to 60 percent in the developing countries.

Even if there are social signs showing important and sure progress, and even if certain fundamental gaps between the south and the north are decreasing, the economic signs are entirely different and drastically negative.

The per-capita income has more than doubled for the industrialized countries in the 1986–87 period.

In the early eighties, the rich countries had $5,000 per inhabitant. By 1990, we had reached $12,000. The developing countries went from $500 to $600, with an increase of 20 percent.

There are no signs that can make us hope for real solid reductions in this economic gap for the future.

General perspectives on world economic development for the next decade are far from being encouraging. A serious development incentive is all that would be needed to exploit the many resources available in the developing countries, even in the most desperate parts of the world.

Therefore, we would like to analyze the United Nations' role in promoting growth, and find a solution in terms of cooperation and interdependence among the numerous nations and governments with different development levels.

Various developing nations have, thanks to us too, managed to increase their collective goods; however, they have also accumulated expensive debts.

In addition, an increasing number of countries of the south and east of the world have acknowledged political civilian rights, chosen the democratic path and accepted working rights and market rights.

But in this world where freedom and democracy are more and more present everywhere, a more meaningful economic cooperation is needed to act as an encouraging and stimulatng element for development and social-political stability.

The transition from an authoritarian collectivism to a market economy, also from headlong "shock therapies" and consequent contradictory actions, is creating worrying social consequences in the East, in the ex–Soviet Union, and even in unified Germany.

According to an EEC group of experts examining the "European Union," in a decade unemployment could be 20 percent in the ex-USSR and in the Eastern countries, and probably in the former East Germany too.

Some continents don't seem to find the strength to overcome the burden of the debt and all the destruction caused by past wars.

In fact, another source less optimistic than WEFA—directed by the

Craxi presenting study to the General Assembly of UN

Craxi, Sec. General De Cuellar, and Rev. Leon Sullivan

Craxi leaving the Glass Palace after receiving his study's approval

Craxi conferring with G-7 world leaders

Craxi in private conference with George Bush of USA

Craxi in private conference with King Fahd of Saudi Arabia

Craxi in private conference with De Cuellar of UN

**Craxi in private conference with Boutros Ghalli of UN**

Craxi meeting in June, 1990, with Japan's leading bankers

**Craxi pictured with leaders of the European Community**

Kein Nobel Award—believes that after the 2 percent fall of the annual per capita product of the eighties, there will be in our present decade an unchanged per-capita product in Africa, and in the first decade of the next century an annual growth equal only to 0.3 percent. However, Latin America—where various countries have done everything possible to come out of the crisis—because of the high inflation rate, because of the low world economic dynamics and the consequent hard-earned development of exports, will reach only in 1995 the per-capita income it had at the end of the seventies.

In Asia alone, because of Japan, growth is expected to take a very positive trend: of course, Japan will have to continue its economic dynamics and China will have to continue to open up to international relations. Under these conditions, a new coordinating and spurring role on behalf of the United Nations in the world economic development and cooperation for a new political equilibrium and regional aggregations is crucial.

This context makes it indispensable for the rich countries to take a greater commitment towards the less developed countries.

As I have said a number of times, the OECD has stated that the donor countries should double the current 0.35 percent rate of their gross product. The World Bank must be provided with financial resources at concessionary conditions, through funds made available by the International Monetary Fund, in order to carry out large concessionary financing operations where necessary to reach recovery and to support development.

Certainly, peace is still very threatened. While threats are placated in a specific area, they can arise in other regions. But the goal set in the preamble of the United Nations' Charter of protecting the future generations from world wars, which twice in the twentieth century have given "unspeakable" pain, seems to have altogether been achieved.

Nevertheless, poverty, hunger, disease, and ignorance are scourges which haven't, to this day, been defeated for too many human beings. Meanwhile, the rate of population has increased, and environmental damage has become more serious.

It is now clear that progress is possible in these areas only by promoting a higher and more consistent development. To achieve this, the "invisible role" of the market is not enough. A more significant effort of world and regional cooperation and coordination is needed, one in which each will do its share, and feel part of the United Nations.

# Report on the Developing Countries' Debt and Growth

# Contents

*Introduction and Main Conclusions*     87
*Preface*     91

Part I: The Great Challenge     94
  I. The Debt Crisis and Underdevelopment     94
    A. The Debt, the Rich, the Poor     94
      1. Why the debt problem concerns us all.     94
      2. Imbalances between the rich and the poor of the world.     96
    B. The Causes and Factors of the Crisis     98
      1. The causes for the pathological growth of the debt.     98
      2. The crisis.     101
      3. The decline of GNP growth in the indebted countries.     102
  II. The Debt and Economic Recovery     103
    A. The Quantitative Parameters     103
      1. The link between debt service, GNP, and export.     103
      2. The link between interest rate and export GNP growth rate.     103
    B. General Political Elements to Overcome the Crisis     104
      1. Steady GNP and export growth.     104
      2. Restraining interest rates and increasing national savings.     104
      3. Fiscal and accounting regulations favorable to the LDCs.     105
      4. New resources and greater aid to development.     105
    C. East European Countries     106
      1. The size of the debt and of the investments of the East European countries.     106
      2. The rapidity and significance of the adjustment process.     107

|     |     |
| --- | --- |
| 3. The risks of further debt. | 107 |
| Part II: Ways Out of the Crisis | 109 |
| I. The Debt-Reduction Strategy | 109 |
| A. The Brady Plan | 109 |
| 1. Looking for solutions. | 109 |
| II. Private and Official Creditors' Debt Reductions | 110 |
| A. The Brady Plan | 110 |
| 1. A courageous approach in the right direction. | 110 |
| 2. New incoming money and the Brady Plan. | 113 |
| 3. Suggestions for reinforcing the Brady Plan. | 114 |
| B. Lightening the Debt with Official Creditors | 115 |
| 1. The Toronto Plan. | 115 |
| 2. The IMF facilitations. | 116 |
| III. Techniques for a Reduction of the Debt Cost | 117 |
| A. Techniques of Debt Conversion | 117 |
| 1. Debt-to-equity swap. | 117 |
| 2. Debt-to-debt conversion. | 118 |
| B. Buy-Back Transactions | 119 |
| 1. Redemption must be immediate. | 119 |
| 2. Bilateral or multilateral financial assistance is needed to carry out the redemption. | 120 |
| 3. Recapitulation. | 121 |
| IV. Financing Development, New Incoming Money, the New Regional Common Markets | 122 |
| A. Financing Development | 122 |
| 1. Transfers between the rich countries and the under-developed countries. | 122 |
| 2. An international constitution of the public debt. | 123 |
| B. New Financing | 124 |
| 1. A few innovative instruments of new finance. | 124 |
| 2. Direct investments. | 125 |
| 3. The new regional common markets. | 126 |
| V. Suggestions for Regional Areas and Groups of Countries | 127 |
| A. Mediterranean and Sub-Saharan Africa | 127 |
| 1. The intermediate countries of Mediterranean Africa. | 127 |
| 2. The Mediterranean bank for development and new financing. | 127 |

       3. Cuts on official debts for the intermediate countries.  128
       4. Recovery policies.  128
       5. Official creditors' remission of the debt for poorest countries.  129
  B. Latin America and the Caribbean  130
       1. Transfers out of Latin America.  130
       2. Debt and underdevelopment.  131
       3. A recycling and reductions plan.  132
       4. Each country has to do its share.  133
  C. The East European Countries  134
       1. Two possible strategies for transition.  134
       2. The double purposes of our suggestions.  134
VI. A Series of Measures to Lighten the Debt of the Various Categories of Debtor Countries  135

# Introduction and Main Conclusions

The following recommendations are based on the actual situation and on what is already being done to reduce the high cost of indebtedness of the developing countries, and they are intended to suggest possible options for the measures which are being enforced and for any new proposals. In the final chapter of the actual report, these recommendations are listed so as to offer a systematic approach for lightening the debt of the various country groups.

Foremost, the cost of the debt represents a very serious burden for many of the developing countries and a great hindrance for their economic and social growth. This explains the necessity to keep on the path chosen by the seven major industrialized countries in the economic summits (1) to lighten the debt of the LDCs, so as to adapt the effort to their paying capacity and put forward the conditions for future development.

The fundamental principles are based on the following considerations:

1. The problem, if we think of how to get the indebted countries and regions out of the crisis they are facing, is a systematic one and it must be handled by involving all the creditors—not only the banks, but also governments and multilateral organizations.
2. The Brady Plan (2) must be reinforced with major resources and a well-coordinated management through an agency within the International Financial Institutions (IFI), and assisted by those regional banks interested.
3. Following the decisions taken by the Group of Seven during the Toronto summits (option A) and that of Paris, it is possible to obtain still another reduction of the cost, adapted to each single LDC category, according to their own level of development and indebtedness. Such a reduction is obtained

by spreading out the debt over a long period of time (thirty or forty years) and by applying interest rates based on different concessions levels according to the country categories.

4. The poorest countries ("IDA-only" group) would benefit from an annulment of their debt service, through official programs of bilateral aid.

5. In all cases, so as to strengthen the reductions made on bilateral debts, it is necessary to carry out a conversion of payments for interests in counterpart funds in indexed local currency, to finance projects of development, environment protection and human capital exploitation.

6. Definition of a new "intermediate category" which stands between the poorest countries and the average-income countries, aimed at granting and regulating prioritary measures for Toronto-type concessions of spread out payments at reduced interest rates.

7. Commitment to guarantee an adequate flow of public and private resources in favour of the LDCs. This makes it necessary to insist on a 0.7 percent GNP for public aid to development on behalf of the industrialized countries, a figure which was reconfirmed by the DAC Ministerial Council on May 14, 1990.

8. Reaffirmation of the single approaches and of the distinction between the various categories of debts; aid credits; government-guaranteed credits; unguaranteed private credits and credits with International Financial Institutions. In this context, debts owed to International Institutions keep privileges, reinforcing their concessionary instruments and allowing a general financial stability.

9. A need for the LDCs—including the East European countries—to adopt rigorous internal adjustment policies arranged with IFIs. These adjustment measures must focus on favoring development and especially protecting the less favored categories of the population.

10. An impelling need to acquire—through appropriate incentives and planning—more active support on behalf of the banks in terms of reducing the interest rates on debts of a

private nature; fiscal and accounting improvements of the industrialized countries; legislations in favor of the loaning banks which will apply such reductions and provide new financial flows for the LDCs.

11. The possibility of increasing the IFI resources is also to be taken into account, together with the SDR (Special Drawing Rights) accredited to the industrialized countries, which the latter will use to finance funds to be used for transactions related to the Brady Plan; in particular, to increase the reductions and facilitations on interests and for bridging transactions.

12. In many indebted countries already endowed with an industrial structure or rich in natural resources, "swap" transactions should be further encouraged, by forming mixed companies and having foreign capital participate in the privatized state companies, as well as BTO (build transfer operate) and BOT (build operate transfer) transactions and commodity bonds, includng these in the "government guaranteed" category. Some other innovative formulas should also be taken into consideration, such as the payment of a part of the public debt service with indexed local bonds on exported goods with the faculty to use such bonds to acquire shares and other securities ("debt-equity service swap").

13. Acknowledgement of that special effort must be taken for the Eastern countries, to help them through financings in the transition phase, so as to encourage a rapid passage towards a market economy without any serious social inconveniences. For purposes of containing the accumulated debt, consideration should be given to conversions of the debt into shares of denationalized companies ("debt-equity swap").

The major cost for the public balances of concessions on bilateral credit is equal to 0.1 percent of the GNP of the industrialized countries: which makes the percentage of public aid to development on the industrialized countries' GNP jump from 0.35 percent to 0.45 percent.

In order to foster development plans, special attention should be given to the formation and strengthening of the regional banks. After the recent constitution of the BERS, it is advisable to create a bank for the Mediterranean region which will permit exploitation of the area's resources, a relaunching of the bordering countries, and thus come to a solution for a number of problems, among which are the population increase and the emigration flows.

# Preface

Four elements in the way of peace and world development for the years to come: (a) wars, (b) poverty, (c) the debt, and (d) environmental degradation.

All these elements are strongly connected. The high level of foreign indebtedness accrued by the less developed countries (LDCs) is in part the result of excessive military expenditure for the purchase of war material. The LDCs' expenditures for defense have gone up six times between 1960 and 1985 because of the lack of political and military security in many areas of the developing world. In fact, while détente has finally become the primary topic in international politics of the industrialized countries of the West and East, conversely, in many developing areas of the South, instability has grown seriously.

The events of the seventies and eighties show that, within the LDCs, the lack of national and international security is intensified by the loose fluctuation of prices in raw materials (with crude products first on the list), and the LDCs' attempts to control their sources of supplies have made everything worse.

All this is clearly represented by the events in the Middle East and by the Persian Gulf crisis of the last months, by their impact on military deployment, by the raw products' prices, interest rates, migrating flows, by labourers' remittances and financial systems of the entire world.

In the eighties, oil, food, and inexpensive raw materials did greatly benefit the industrialized countries, but exporters had to sell their products at lower prices than they previously did, while their imports became more expensive; they were neither able to pay their debts nor to carry out investments to fight poverty. In Africa and Latin America, development stopped and poverty went up in the last decade.

Poverty generates environmental degradation both in rural areas and in urban ones: in the first, the high consumption of wood—the greatest source of energy in many regions struck by poverty—causes desertification; in the second, urban misery can only cause decay, even where basic services and infrastructures are provided for. The World Bank's most recent assessments prove that poverty in the LDCs is spreading at a rate which is higher than that of the population growth. This impoverishment leads to political instability. Debt, war, poverty and deterioration of our common good are all linked to one another; dealing with one of these topics means dealing with every single one of them. They are all part of the same political tragedy of the nineties.

The political and economic events of the recent months should make us more aware of the frequency and of the seriousness of the local conflicts and of their expansion within the whole international territory.

They are a clear indication of the need to promote cooperation at an international level with the purpose of stopping this very vicious circle of war-debt-poverty-environmental degradation. They also indicate the necessity to focus on lightening the debt service and on financial concessions to those countries which show a respect for human rights, fight for peace, and work out valid plans for recovery and development.

Previous evaluations indicate that in the immediate future, prospects for the LDCs in general are worsening because of the slowing down of the industrialized countries' growth, because of the higher interest rates and because of the price increases of raw products.

Before the Gulf crisis, an improvement was expected in the LDCs in terms of real growth rate of the GDP, from 3.2 percent in 1990 to 4.2 percent in 1991, principally because of the good harvests and the steady expansion (5.1 percent) of two large low-income countries: China and India. Many of the LDCs were expected to benefit from the structural adjustment plans they had tried hard to obtain.

Preliminary evaluations of the crisis impact on the Gulf suggest a half of a percentage point reduction of the growth rate of the industrial market economies. According to a quantitative study of the effects on the LDCs, the situation will be even worse than expected. Moreover, the increase of interest rates and the restrictions on the growth of liquidity worldwide would strike all the LDCs without exceptions, including the few which produce and export raw materials. The benefits obtained by those few countries, from the price increase of the crude products, is seriously affected by the cost of the interest-rate increase which all must bear.

In brief, a local conflict with widespread international ramifications means:

- Stagnation or even a negative per-capita growth rate for many low-income countries, especially in Africa;
- Creating strong indebtedness for large countries with low income in south Asia, which had not had, up to now, serious debt problems;
- Increasing the burden of the debt of a number of low-average-income countries;
- Adding new pressure to the severe difficulties of the balances of payments of the East and Central European countries, and
- Curtailing the flow of foreign funds to those seriously indebted countries (like Mexico and Nigeria) which export raw materials.

This is a type of conflict which puts in danger the structural readjustment of those countries where attempts have been made to promote new policies. Moreover, it is most likely to produce greater poverty and risks for the environment.

1. The proposals in this report are geared to focus on the necessity of reducing the debt burden of the LDCs. They are the result of studies and consultations with the leaders of industrialized and developing countries as well as with the financial community. These proposals aim at relieving both the debt burden and one of the causes fostering conflicts, poverty and environmental degradation. They are not to be taken as technical solutions to problems of financial engineering; they are proposals which aim at reaching a solution for those most significant political and social issues connected to the world development of the nineties.

# Part I

# The Great Challenge

## I. The Debt Crisis and Underdevelopment

### A. The Debt, the Rich, the Poor

*1. Why the debt problem concerns us all.*

    a. It is often said that the debt problem of the developing countries only concerns those specific countries. But in spite of the good prospects of the last few years, its impact on the industrialized countries has been very strong.

    b. However, as it has been observed, the debt problem is very tightly linked to wars, poverty, and environmental degradation. Drug traffic, emigration from countries which are oppressed by a stagnant economy, the environmental issue, unbalanced trade, and political instability are all phenomena that are rendered more serious by ill development and by the unsolved and worsened debt paralysis of the last years.

    c. The issue concerning the chaotic migrating flow from Latin America to the northern part of the hemisphere is often a desperate act, not a choice. A similar problem concerns the European countries that have to deal with the African issue. The only alternative to such flows of immigrants depends on development, something which is only possible if the debt burden is curtailed.

    d. The drug issue is also tightly connected with the solution to the debt problem of the less developed countries: in strongly indebted countries, drug cultivation and drug traffic represent a sort of remedy to underdevelopment, which is difficult to eradicate in those countries that live in true economic frustration and degradation. This kind of an issue can and must be fought against by substituting an unhealthy economic system with a healthy one; otherwise some countries will continue to rely on drug cultivation. Some extremist social and political tendencies are even generated by poverty and deprivation.

e. The environmental question is also tightly linked to poverty and debt. In fact, the desperate search for land to deforest for pasturage and low-standard farming, the improper use of lands in the underdeveloped countries of Latin America, Asia and Africa, and desertification caused by a lack of irrigation and a missing alternative to wood are essentially due to an economic decline and paralysis.

f. This means an abnormal pressure of the population on the natural resources cannot be controlled or limited without the adequate tools of a developing economy. Besides, development and ecology are two problems impossible to solve if the debt service absorbs a great share of the national resources and taxes.

g. The forced export flow from countries which must pay their debts might have, at times, aroused protectionist tendencies and negative repercussions on multilateral negotiations for the liberalization of world trade.

h. Yet another worrying question should concern us all: the debt crisis of the developing countries and the East European countries has placed major international financial institutions like the World Bank and the International Monetary Fund in a very fragile situation.

i. New loans to indebted countries can be a trap for the World Bank, difficult to overcome without participation from the greatest part of the creditors. On the other hand, simply offering loans only to those countries which don't present any risk would mean not complying with the role of a bank devoted to development.

j. The same is true for the International Monetary Fund, which grants loans to countries at such a cost that it pushes them on the edge of survival and places these countries in a dangerous position. In such situations, these countries often stop paying and accumulate debts with the IMF and the other official creditors.

k. The recent increase of the IMF shares is to be considered an instrument to furnish new means to the LDCs and particularly to relieve their debt burden. As positive a step as this may be, it remains insufficient to solve the debt problem which has gone out of proportion. It would be necessary to investigate the possibility of further increasing the International Monetary Fund's commitment and that of other multilateral financial institutions in regard to granted resources to be used for debt reductions and debt service transactions. From this point of view, it is interesting to consider the proposal of carrying out a special SDR issuance to be used as a guarantee for the payment of interests on the debentures issued by the developing countries as conversions of their commercial debt.

l. Because the debt of the less developed countries takes place in a context of interdependencies, it is now obvious that it does not only concern the debtor countries. It is an issue that implicates us all and could well undermine the industrialized countries' economies and the multilateral institutions' financial stability if a suitable solution is not reached through common action.

## 2. *Imbalances between the rich and the poor of the world.*

a. The debt problem we are analyzing is not a simple relation problem between creditors and debtors. A billion people, living in countries that are oppressed by the debt, live in conditions of poverty.

b. Almost 70 percent of the world product is produced and

consumed by 15 percent of the population. The Third World countries, with 76 percent of the world population, have less than 20 percent of the world revenue. In 1987, the per-capita income in the poorest countries (with a population of 2.8 billion) amounted to $290, versus the $14,500 of the advanced countries belonging to a market economy. These poorest countries had half of the world population, and only 5.6 percent of the world income.

c. In the poor countries of Africa and South America, the daily per-capita intake of calories is 2,385, while in the industrial countries it is 3,375. Life expectancy is forty-seven in many black African countries, while it is seventy-seven in the rich countries of the West.

d. Decisions (or lack of decision) on behalf of the industrialized countries naturally have a strong impact on the LDCs. The extraordinary increase of the real interest rate of the eighties has once more shown this "power" of influencing the lives of the poor countries.

e. The long-term interest rate of the seven major industrialized countries for all the decades following the Second World War has never gone beyond 4 percent. It may have been negative or near zero at a time in the seventies when some industrialized countries initially answered with inflationary policies to the increase of raw materials in 1973: as a result, the world financial reserves expanded rapidly and the inflationary pressure increased. It was in the first half of the eighties that the macroeconomic stabilization was brought about almost exclusively through anti-inflationary monetary policies. Without the help of adequate fiscal and income policies, the result was an increase of the real interest rates above 5 percent in most of the industrialized countries.

f. Later, this increase was kept at high levels by (1) the constant balance deficits in some important industrialized countries, (2) the reduction of savings rates in most of these countries, and (3) the greater production of investments which come with an increased productivity in the OECD.

## B. The Causes and Factors of the Crisis

*1. The causes for the pathological growth of the debt.*

    a. Between 1980 and 1990 the external debt in the developing countries grew rapidly and, according to Bretton Woods' Institutions, it now amounts to $1,200 billion. At the same time, the flow of payments for interests and repayment of debt passed from about $90 billion in 1980 to the $180 billion expected for 1990.

    b. There are different causes for the increase of this enormous debt, just as there are great differences from one country to the next. However, in most cases, the external debt was created by the developing countries to finance the balance deficit involved in the financing of development plans.

    c. Public investments were often selected and carried out in a poor manner. The profitability, in economic and social terms, of a number of projects was low, even if these were financed with borrowed resources at high rates of interest. Besides, the national institutions had to bear enormous responsibility for having left the prominent power of decision to the government's democracies which chose to finance public investments by creating public debt.

    d. The profitability of investments would have been much higher if they had been undertaken by private or public enterprises, endowed with autonomous management of financial responsibility. At times, the low productivity was caused by all the energy placed in economic regimes purely imitating collectivistic systems in bureaucratic planning.

    e. On the other hand, this external debt was often contracted to finance the balance of payments deficit, which was linked to the balance deficit of the public sector. The serious worsening of the LDCs' commercial exportations we witnessed in the eighties was one of the main causes for the debt deterioration.

f. One of the fundamental causes of the abnormal development of the foreign debt in the developing countries lies in the absence of what could be depicted as an "international monetary and fiscal constitution." There was no rule or international agreement that directed or coordinated the issue of international public debt. As a consequence, the debt became extremely risky for the LDCs.

g. On the other hand, in the late seventies the banks of the developed countries were driven by the abundant money that followed the oil-producing countries' surplus as well as the optimal conditions they could obtain, and were not stopped by the inspection bodies of their original countries. Therefore, they expanded their loan programs in the LDCs beyond measure.

h. In those times, the price increase of raw materials was seen as a new reality doomed to last, and not as a cyclic phenomenon. This induced creditors and debtors to behave irrationally. The price increase of oil of the second half of the seventies led to euphoric international financial and insurance initiatives toward these countries; the creditors' way of handling the matter is now perceived as strongly irrational, even if it seemed rational then.

i. All the countries now in debt were then granted generous warranties by the public insurance organizations of the industrial countries who wished to benefit from convenient supplies and advantageous business conditions.

j. Given the lack of monetary and fiscal international rules, a public or private transactor loaned without knowing how much had already been loaned or how much other countries intended to loan. As long as another country had granted a loan to these countries on the basis of their natural resources, especially oil-wise, the old debts could be paid thanks to new loans. But an end had to come for this spiral.

k. When prices of the raw materials collapsed, it was initially thought that the phenomenon was only a temporary one and new foreign debts were contracted so as to finance consumptions and the balance of payments deficit. Thus the adjustment process was pushed back in time and the debt problem became more serious. Nevertheless, at that time, no industrialized country offered help.

l. Even if for the consequences of the 1986 fall of the dollar and for the 1987 collapse of the world stock, generous financial "dampers" were set, the situation turned to be entirely different in the case of excessive credit, which was granted to the less developed countries in the late seventies.

m. On the contrary, no consideration was given to the serious repercussions that the real interest rates growth had on the LDCs. Surely, these countries also have a great share of responsibility in this matter.

n. Many of them had and still have, with the high public expenditure, low fiscal pressure, which in certain countries is due to acquired interests, in others to the inheritance of bad managing, and in others it is simply the consequence of a poor institutional basis. There are many possible "therapies," but all should take into account that a healthy fiscal administration is the basis of any adjustment program.

o. At last, it should not be forgotten that the long crisis period of the LDCs is due to the extremely high demographic pressure and to its negative effects on the accrual and on the environment: there can be no long-lasting solution to the debt and development problems without following through with demographic policies.

## 2. The crisis.

a. In this complex situation, many LDCs got trapped into a state of deep crisis where the ever-changing political sceneries caused a series of depreciations and appreciations of the exchange rates, together with attempts at trade liberalizations which were often overturned in the same way they had been adopted. Government policies often lost credibility, thus leading to a number of inflationary patterns, with the consequent decline of the GNP. It became more and more difficult for most of the LDCs to face their own foreign debt.

b. In some others, the cost of the debt soon reached such levels that the banks began to suspect bankruptcy and became more and more reluctant to grant new loans. This logical worry was soon confirmed by the request of the central bank authorities to increase the potential loss reserves vis-à-vis the LDCs. Another deterrent element in the offer of new loans to these countries was the growth of a secondary market which caused the diminution of the debt quotations of the LDCs.

c. The high level of prudential provisions for losses made necessary by the debt crises of the developing countries was effected by the international banking system, on the basis of fiscal and banking regulations which, on the whole, favored such provisions, thereby reducing the need to concede reductions of old debt or new loans. It involved a real vicious cycle, because the loss provisions acted as a deterrent against the debt cuts or new financial flows towards the LDCs.

d. The massive loss provisions on the part of the lead banks have made evident the conviction that certain countries were no longer solvent. This blocked their loans and rendered them even less solvent. As a consequence, the value of their debt in the secondary market fell, thus further blocking their credibility for obtaining new loans.

3. *The decline of GNP growth in the indebted countries.*

   a. The severely indebted countries' GNP and export rates are generally low, compared to those of the other LDCs. And imports decrease instead of increasing.

**Growth and Investments in the LDCs, 1982–89
(Percentages)**

|  | Very indebted | | Other |
|---|---|---|---|
|  | Average income | Low income |  |
| GNP | 1.4 | 0.8 | 6.4 |
| Investment rate | 19.8 | 13.1 | 27.5 |
| Export growth rate | 4.9 | 1.1 | 8.3 |
| Import growth rate | -0.2 | -6.8 | 5.5 |

*Source: International Monetary Fund. Growth rates are expressed in real terms.*

   b. Naturally, there is an economic limit to the paying capacity. While in the case of an enterprise oppressed by debts, bankruptcy or an estimate arranged with all creditors can often allow for new loans, in the case of the debtor countries there is no international financial constitution establishing such rule.
   c. From his own initiative, the single creditor has no interest in conceding a solid discount on his own credit and new loans. This would increase the paying capacity of the debtor, for all his loans, including his loans with other creditors, generating "external economies" to their benefit. But what would be advantageous for creditors globally isn't for the single creditor.
   d. A legislative coordination between debtors and creditors, which is often guaranteed by bankruptcy laws within a country, cannot be reached at an international level without constituting a group of laws that are accepted universally.
   e. Of course, there must be an institution endowed with incentives to carry out the collective agreements which don't become concrete spontaneously. In this frame of mind, each has to do his share.

## II. The Debt and Economic Recovery

### A. The Quantitative Parameters

*1. The link between debt service, GNP, and export.*

    a. The tremendous weight of the debt service on national income and exports implies burdensome transfers of resources destined for consumption and for internal investments.

    b. The diminution of available means on behalf of the national community towards the LDCs has become drastic because of the lowering of the average income and because of the disproportions between incomes.

    c. Since a large share of the developing countries' debt is public debt, its financing implies tax increases, cuts on expenses or further issue of debt, or to transfer the deficit, with inflation, onto the whole of the economy.

    d. If the debt service represents a share of exportation which is too high, not only will it be necessary to limit imports through strict tributary measures and to put monetary brakes on credit requests, but other unhealthy and discriminating measures will have to be taken: import duty, dues on imports and credits. This will have repercussions on the standard of living and on investment, thus putting political and social stability as well as the growth process of economy and employment in danger.

*2. The link between interest rate and export GNP growth rate.*

    a. Two elements are fundamental in order to solve the debt problem: First, the growth rate of the gross product of the indebted country, measured in the currency in which the debt is declared, must be slightly superior to the interest rate which is expressed in such currency. Obviously, if new debts are not contracted, besides those due

to an accumulation of unpaid interests, the stock of the debt in this case will slowly become a smaller percentage of the gross product of the indebted country.
b. The second condition is that the growth rate of net exportations will have to grow higher than the interest rate.
c. Keeping these two results in mind, one can understand why in the eighties the problem of the debt worsened. In fact, on average, the interest rate went beyond the GNP growth rate and the growth rate of exportations was below the interest rate for the developing countries which now are in trouble.

## B. General Political Elements to Overcome the Crisis

*1. Steady GNP and export growth.*

a. After having closely studied the debt problem and having discussed it with the leaders of the creditor and debtor governments and within the financial community overall, two points were agreed on unanimously. The first one is that the debt can only be solved in a climate of total growth, and therefore in the debtor country as much as in the creditor country.
b. Secondly, it is necessary that the debt problem of the developing countries be linked—generally or specifically—to the possible expansion of export and to the stabilizing of prices of goods and services which those countries export in the world markets.

*2. Restraining interest rates and increasing national savings.*

a. In the industrialized countries, strict monetary, fiscal and income policies must be adopted in order to neutralize inflation tendencies and maintain the interest rates at a low level during the nineties. All this is very important, especially in light of the developments of

August and September of this year, which focus on further growth of interest rates. This is something that could have severe consequences on the debt problem and on the countries' growth.

b. Indebted countries need healthy finance and true market economy measures and rules in order to increase their savings rate, attract domestic and foreign investment, increase investment productivity, and create a framework of political and institutional certainties. All this must be done to allow a steadier growth of the national product.

c. However, the developing countries' self-determination in carrying out these changes must be respected. In fact, these must be based on (1) incitement, when possible, of the market force, (2) international cooperation, and (3) a gradual application of the changes, so as to prevent social phenomena that could endanger the growth process.

d. Policies of "adjustment" must not overlook the human side of the unexpected price increases and cuts in public spending. Efforts must be made to protect the most vulnerable groups from unfair privations. Adjustments must not be seen in ideologic terms, but more as a necessary step towards modernization and restoration of economic cooperation between the debtor countries and their creditors.

*3. Fiscal and accounting regulations favorable to the LDCs.*

a. A systematic approach requires one essential element, that of reviewing fiscal, accounting, and control norms of the central bank authorities, so as to facilitate instead of obstructing cuts of the developing countries' debt.

*4. New resources and greater aid to development.*

a. It is indispensable for the growth in the developing countries to be sustained by a policy of the Western countries and of their organizations which will offer the necessary public aid for development. There should be an increase of official aid for development at the 0.70 percent level of the GNP that the DAC believes to be necessary in order to relaunch economic growth.

b. A revival of the growth process will be allowed only if the debt reduction is accompanied by immediate interventions. Commercial credit and public insurances, just like regional banks and multilateral institutions, have a very important role to play in this field. Of course, in order to carry out these initiatives, they will also need special concessions, besides bank resources.

c. In the end, all this will put to a test the industrialized world taxpayer who will have to show greater wisdom in the joint responsibility for the tragedy of underdevelopment. This involves a clear political commitment, besides all the efforts in terms of technique and financial engineering that may be brought out.

## C. East European Countries

*1. The size of the debt and of the investments of the East European countries.*

a. At the end of 1988, the size of the East European countries' debt (besides the USSR) amounted to $100 billion, of which 40 percent was Poland's and 20 percent Hungary's.

b. The bureaucratic and economic planning system, a centralized and substantially monopolitical one, has turned out unable to replace the flexibility of organization and productivity of the market system. The lack of an open economy has countries of an important advanced industrial tradition in Eastern Europe, such as Czechoslovakia and Eastern Germany, as well as countries with a strong agricultural background and average industry like Hungary, on the wane.

c. This is what happened in spite of capital accumulation and because of the drop in productivity. Between 1974 and 1984, productivity in the USSR went down 1.4 percent annually, while it went up 1.3 percent annually in the industrialized countries; work productivity only went up 1 percent versus 2.7 percent in the industrialized countries. The trend in the East European countries was similar.

2. *The rapidity and significance of the adjustment process.*

   a. Much work has to be done still, the first reason probably being that the aims to be reached in a medium term have not yet been clearly decided. Besides, there is considerable progress in today's enterprises, which offer better quality, adapt the product to the market in a better way, increase profit and develop the company's finance in an efficient manner.
   b. Partial reforms enforced in some of these countries in the seventies and eighties have in some cases made problems worse, by loosening payments and general rules of the plan without offering in exchange incentives and autonomy that will lead to greater efficiency and competition. Therefore, inflation pressures were made worse.

3. *The risks of further debt.*

   a. In terms of financings, we can clearly see that these countries don't have a problem of quantity but rather one of quality. Inefficiency could be the consequence of too great a number of financings without a careful selection. This has often been the case with state enterprises, which operated for long periods of time without any management links and in the certainty that any losses would be replaced by the state and financed by making sacrifices on the collectivities' life standards or by raising foreign indebtedness.

b. Remarkable progress was achieved in recent years in the European East's advance towards a market economy: courageous changes in planning, in prices, changes, organization of capital markets, work and services, and strengthening of public finance.

# Part II
# Ways Out of the Crisis

## I. The Debt-Reduction Strategy

### A. The Brady Plan

*1. Looking for solutions.*

    a. Ever since the early eighties, the international community has looked for solutions to the debt issue. Three phases of this process can be outlined as follows:
      (1) Up until 1985, market solutions were always strongly emphasized; that is, some kind of financial strategy to prevent new debt accumulation.
      (2) From 1985 until March 1989, research of financial resources in favor of the severely indebted countries was the main focus, so as to foster growth and structural recovery and reduce their debt burden (the "Baker Plan," named after the former American secretary of state).
      (3) Curtailing the debt has been the main concern since 1989.
    b. In the following chapters, I will examine the progress achieved through the debt-reduction strategy as well as the specific techniques to reduce the debt burden. Subsequently, I will discuss financial developments and developments of the regional cooperation, also giving personal suggestions for each regional area and group of countries.

## II. Private and Official Creditors' Debt Reductions

### A. The Brady Plan

*1. A courageous approach in the right direction.*

    a. The Brady Plan explicitly acknowledges that it is necessary not only to reduce the bank debt, but also to manage a consistent bank intervention of the IMF and the World Bank so as to reduce the debt. It considers this reduction to be even more advantageous to the creditors than to the debtors and therefore within reach through a voluntary agreement between both sides. It also acknowledges that the indebted countries need new currency. Here is how the Brady Plan is composed:
      (1) financings from official sources to support reductions of debt service;
      (2) conversion of the short-to-average-term debt in long-term debt and/or ordinary actions;
      (3) debt payment;
      (4) general agreement between country (or countries) and debtor(s) and the loaning banks, on the basis of credible and possible adjustment programs.
    b. In spite of its positive impact in some cases, the implementation of the Brady Plan has brought out a series of problems linked to the length of negotiations, the lack of funds, and the use of guarantees. There are many explanations to the lengthy negotiations of the Brady Plan on the debt problem. The first is that, because of contractual reasons, there is a mutual double interference between banks. Generally, these banks, being members of loaning associations, are all connected through the "sharing" clause that requires any of the banks getting a certain benefit to split it up proportionally among all the others. Banks are usually linked by the "negative pledge" clause: it is not possible to satisfy a certain credit obtained subsequently if the one pre-

viously obtained hasn't been satisfied. The presence of these clauses and the lacking availability shown by the crediting banks have made the Brady Plan negotiations lengthy and willing to accept lower concessions than the ones initially intended. Therefore, this new debt strategy must be reinforced through creation of legal and institutional mechanisms necessary to grant good coordination between all the parts concerned with debt-reduction transactions.

c. The Brady Plan's available financial resources level is probably inadequate to carry out all the wanted reductions, and at the wanted speed. They are also insufficient to stimulate new financial flows towards the countries that are included in the recovery plan.

d. Other countries should follow Japan's example of contribution in the recycling plan which provides assistance to the Brady Plan. Otherwise the use of SDR would be necessary to reach the same aim.

e. The reduced guarantee on interests (except for the eighteen months) reduces tremendously the enhancement of bonds issued by the debtor countries for conversion or redemption of the debt. Besides, a large guarantee on the interests could also lead to consideration of larger debt reductions.

f. The Brady Plan's difficulties could be overcome more efficiently, as regards a coordination of the creditor banks and to the resources available, if there were an office or a special body within the Bretton Woods Institution which managed all the aspects of the debt and the transactions regarding service reductions.

g. Another touchy issue in the Brady Plan is the differences between the various national regimes for tax, accounting, and banking regulations with regards to the developing countries. In some countries—Switzerland, Great Britain, Germany, France—the income tax regulations allow a deduction for substantial reserve for doubtful credits from the moment in which they are constituted; in others (Japan, Italy, U.S.A.) such deductions are not allowed unless for a minimal percentage; the loss is allowed as a deduction when realized in the form of a capital loss. These differences in tax treatment provoke distortions and delay the negotiations on the reduction of the debt.

h. In the major part of the countries of the first group, the banking authorities do not permit a write-off of these credits until the legal means of collection have been exhausted. This is the reason why banks are not interested in a reduction of the debt, such transaction not giving them any tax benefit and their risk, however, being covered by the reserves.

i. In countries where the loss is allowed as a deduction, banks haven't always been able to protect themselves with significant reserves, because they cannot use these reserves to reduce taxable profits and improve their balance through a "tax dividend." Neither can they set paying-off over a long period of years. Besides, what interests these banks is capital reductions, but not interest reductions, which usually (even though some changes are being realized here lately) cannot be considered as tax losses.

j. The actual distortions could lead one to think that tax deductions for reserves can be much larger, but they constitute only a tax deferral. If after a certain amount of time, such reserves have not been used to cover credit reductions in established insolvency from creditors, these would be included in their taxation. This could at least be applied to the United States's or Japan's tax systems, and now to the Italian one, these systems no longer allowing provisions of reserves on credits towards doubtful countries.

k. Moreover, certain cases should allow amortizations of acknowleged losses, for accounting purposes, when such losses are found because of reductions or reconversion general transactions, as is the case in the Brady Plan.

l. In the countries where the deduction of the effective losses on debts only is admitted, it would be necessary to also allow the capitalized financial loss deduction which is due to the interests' reductions, so as to insure tax neutrality between the various options of the Brady Plan and increase the overall convenience. The same should be done about the financial charges which derive from the Brady Plan's "new currency" option.

2. *New incoming money and the Brady Plan.*

   a. It is illogical for a large restructurization with guarantees on residual credit not to be reflected in a positive manner on the "country risk" and therefore on the obligation of provisions for new loans. If, aside from the bank debt, the other debts are also converted, the paying capacity increases while the insurance risk for shares resulting from conversion for the new loans decreases.
   b. The search for new funds is another of the cofinancing purposes of the new Expanded Cofinancing Operation (ECO) of the World Bank. This should be available to countries like Colombia which haven't to this date restructured their debt, as well as countries like Mexico and Chile (and soon more countries like Venezuela and Uruguay) which have agreed on the Brady Plan agreements, having accepted the conditions—in terms of economic recovery—which are listed in the plan.
   c. Besides, many commercial banks have repeated their will to operate in the developing countries, as long as incentives are provided for those following this choice. Among the incentives particularly mentioned by the World Bank are: trade-finance facilities, own lending project financing, new money bonds (for which public insurance guarantees would be needed) and cofinancing with the World Bank and regional development banks, like Inter-American Development Bank.

3. *Suggestions for reinforcing the Brady Plan*

   a. The Economic Commission of Latin America and Caribbean, after having noticed that the Brady Plan is "uncoordinated," argues that banks are not likely to give up their requirements and therefore there is a tendency for some banks to pull back:
   "There is no substitute for a coherent institutional framework that makes each country's offer of debt reduction within the context of an officially supported adjustment program one that most banks cannot refuse. The framework must include incentives for good social behaviors and sanctions for anti-social free-riding. The Brady Plan lacks a coherent structure."
   b. In their report on the first results of the Brady Plan, the World Bank and the IMF both admit that, up until now, less agreements than originally expected have been reached. According to them, it is necessary to speed up the procedures, but without damaging the adjustment programs; the vulnerability of the countries whose debt was restructured in the light of future unfavorable situations should not represent an unjust transfer of burden between private and official creditors. Besides, the two organizations declare that governments never made an effort comparable to that required from banks, in terms of official credits granted to the "average income strongly indebted countries," and that even the Toronto Plan is inadequate for the poorest countries. It is necessary that the funds for restructuring of the debt be supplementary, aside from the ones coming from multinational organizations.
   c. According to the World Bank and the IMF, the debtor countries should also encourage (instead of discouraging) direct foreign investment, financing from commercial banks of specific projects and commercial transactions, repatriation of capital. Market-oriented reform measures, including the provision of timely repatriation of dividends, development of local capital

markets, the full protection of domestic courts in case of private default, and the elimination of financial repression and unfair taxation practices are the key elements in this procedure. Special incentives should also be provided to speed up negotiations and to insure that these are fully respected.

## B. Lightening the Debt with Official Creditors

*1. The Toronto Plan.*

    a. The Toronto Plan applied by the Club of Paris—on the basis of the agreements of the G–7 Summit of Toronto—was decided upon and organized during the annual meeting between the World Bank and the IMF in Berlin in 1988, and it concerns the restructuring of debts of the LDCs towards governments of the rich countries. Under this initiative, all debts with replanned paying terms will have a twenty-five-years maturity term, including a fourteen-year tolerance limit. For nonconcessionary debts, the creditor countries will be able to choose payment conditions among three technical alternatives.

      (1) *Partial cancelling.* Cancelling of one-third of the due debt service during the renegotiation, and setting a date for payments in standard terms for the low-income countries (a fourteen-year maturity and an eight-year tolerance period at market interests).

      (2) *Extended maturity.* Setting payment terms of the entire amount of the debt at market interests, but with a twenty-five-year maturity and a fourteen-year tolerance period.

      (3) *Concessionary interest rates.* Resettling payment terms for the whole amount according to the maturity terms of the (1) option, but at a 3.5 percent interest rate, at market rates.

b. This program is not adequate. While in order to promote consistent reductions on the debt burden for all the severely indebted countries the Brady Plan addresses all the commercial banks, the Toronto Plan only addresses the governments of the average indebted poorest nations.

c. For what concerns the nonconcessionary debts towards governments, among all the various alternatives, the option (1) appears to be the most logical to solve the difficulty or impossibility of paying, as it does include the burden reduction of interests. In fact, this option involves the annulment of a third of the maturities and it reprograms the rest with a fourteen-year maturity period, including a tolerance period of eight years. But this option also seems weak for two reasons.

d. As a first thing, the reduction is not sufficient for the poor countries. With the Brady Plan, this reduction has shown to be insufficient to help the severely indebted average-income countries, and very inadequate for the severely indebted poor countries.

e. Besides, the extension of the maturities produces a concentration of obligations for the future, which makes it less easy to come out of the crisis and creates new needs for further restructuring. The accumulation of debt burdens puts the poor indebted countries in the predicament of obtaining further commercial credit and restrains foreign financing of investments, obstructing that payment to the market, which is considered fundamental by the adjustment plans. The weak point of all the Toronto options, as can be easily seen in the diagram below, is the increase of the future cost of the debt service.

2. *The IMF facilitations.*

a. At the end of 1987, the IMF established the ESAF (enhanced structural adjustment facility) to help low-income countries with protracted problems in their balance of payments to adjust their policies and reach, in an average term period, better growth. This program was united with the SAF (Structural Adjustment Facility), established in March of 1986. Now the two plans put together provide about $12 billion (11.7) in ten-year credits, at the highly advantageous rate of 0.5 percent, with a five-year tolerance period (about two-thirds for ESAF and one-third for SAF).

b. Without this support and the special interventions from the World Bank, which we examined in the first part of this report, the picture would not be just bad, but tragic. But the partial shares are not sufficient; in fact, they don't handle the debt burden issue in a direct manner.

c. Similar considerations are true for the World Bank's credits. The international financial institutions should obtain more concessionary funds for aims different than the usual ones.

d. The IMF and World Bank lightening the debt and the arrears of these institutions are not issues that only concern the poor countries, but also the average-income ones.

## III. Techniques for a Reduction of the Debt Cost

### A. Techniques of Debt Conversion

*1. Debt-to-equity swap.*

a. The debt-for-equity swaps linked to privatizations—even if partial—and relaunching projects of local enterprise, should be considered in the context of a modernizing policy and one of genuine liberalization, deregulation, and unbureaucratization of the economy.

b. It is not simply a question of developing capital flow to eliminate the foreign debt, but more an interest in linking the debt restructuring policy to the issue of economic recovery.

c. A study of the World Bank shows that the debt-conversion investments in shares definitely favored the enterprises operating in the sector of exportation. Foreign investment—at least in mixed companies or commercial companies—helps to get rid of existing barriers for importation in the industrialized countries.

d. Therefore, the debt-for-equity swap could be an outpost of "new finance" flows towards the economic initiatives of indebted countries and lead to new exportation on behalf of these countries.

2. *Debt-to-debt conversion.*

a. Among the restructuring transactions that include some kind of alleviation, the ones which particularly interest us are those that will limit the burdensomeness of the Libor plus interest rate, often contracted when the indebted countries' prices of raw materials were higher or when the market real-interest rate was lower.

b. Nevertheless, a simple passage from Libor plus to a fixed interest rate might not offer any advantage if it is not fixed through especially favorable criteria. Restructurings that are brought about during peak interest-rate periods could generate fixed rates which, subsequently, might be higher than the market rate. One of the solutions to this problem would be a variable-rate ceiling. In order to increase its potential benefit, this ceiling should be established at a highly discounted level.

c. Besides, it is necessary to consider the proposal of matching the debt service to the prices of basic necessities exported from the debtor countries. With this mechanism, the paying possibility of the debtor countries will not be conditioned by the unfavorable fluctuations in the world markets trade.

d. There are two types of debt conversion that could be adantageous for the debtors, and this with a limited cost for creditors, as long as a sufficiently high number of creditors join the program. The first one is the provision of unpaid interests in an account that will be at the debtor's expense, without an arrears indemnity, and only at a low cost for the extention that is granted. The second one consists in paying a part of the debt service in local currency.

e. The first formula makes sense only if the country in question has a substantial capacity to pay in the long run and if, each year, it manages—through help from the international institutions—to pay off a part of its debt that is higher than the unpaid interests.

f. According to another type of conversion of the debt, total or partial payment of the debt burden must be made in indexed local currency to a basket of commodities, to be used for the purchase of goods in the debtor country.

## B. Buy-Back Transactions

*1. Redemption must be immediate.*

a. The voluntary buy-back of foreign debt from the debtor countries, when its quotation in the secondary market is low, can be a very attractive operation. But if extended and prolonged, this transaction ends up being harmful; as with debt institutional buyers present in the secondary market, the debt goes up in price. Besides, a country deciding on its own buy-back in the secondary market can be tempted to have contradicting behaviours which would discourage new currency flows.

b. Indeed, an indebted country that, in the face of payment difficulties, carries out a de facto moratorium of its debt discourages the flow of new loans and holds down flows in the secondary market.

c. Therefore, redemption should be carried out in big

shares, through transactions agreed on once and for all and with a price that is established in advance.

d. Just like in the case of a conversion into shares (which we discussed previously), redemption requires consensus from the crediting banks. One can expect the banks to behave as "free riders" when they are waiting—because of redemptions on debts being effected with other banks—for the price to go up. To avoid this kind of behaviour, it will be necessary that the purchase prices offered be blocked, at predetermined levels.

e. For this reason, too, an agreement based on objective criteria and within a clear institutional agreement seems the only possible way to reach a large-scale redemption.

*2. Bilateral or multilateral financial assistance is needed to carry out the redemption.*

a. A redemption is almost always a public finance transaction, since the greatest part of debts was contracted by central governments and other public finance institutions or by public enterprises guaranteed by governments. So as to effect a buy-back, a single government can be assisted by some loan from an international institution.

b. If a country seems likely to merit credit again, purchase of the debt with a strong discount on the secondary market should not be considered, as it could have negative consequences on potential flows of new finances.

c. Instead, those countries that are far from remeriting credit and which, after having undergone great political changes (i.e., general elections bringing a return to democracy), finally have a credible government, find themselves in an extremely fragile position.

d. Entirely repudiating their predecessors' debt will surely damage their credibility. It is wiser for them to show willingness to pay a sum which will be adjusted to their own paying capability and to the value that—in presence of the previous government—the debt had reached on the secondary market. Let's say that when not assisted through international financings allowing global transactions, redemption could be revealed to be more advantageous to creditors than to debtors.

e. Aid from financial or bilateral organizatons seems an essential "ingredient" to make these transactions successful, as it will:
   (1) help them financially;
   (2) ensure totality;
   (3) establish that even if the redemption has developed gradually, its price of reference is that of the initial period when the global negotiation took place.

## 3. *Recapitulation.*

a. To conclude, in order to increase the possibility of cuts on the debt burden, the following measures are strongly advised:
   (1) Increasing the public resources according to the Brady Plan so as to increase the level of the reduction of the debt and/or of the debt cost to 50 percent.
   (2) Ensuring a neutral handling of the possible options thanks to equivalent guarantees (or other forms of guarantee) on capitals, interests, and new financings, through equivalent fiscal regimes.
   (3) Providing a partial lightening of the debt with indexed accounts expressed in local currency or to be used for purchasing property, shares, and goods.
   (4) Curtailng the necessary reserves that are necessary for the loans guaranteed to countries that have agreed on the debt reduction.
   (5) Forming an official coordinating committee or an organization within international financial institutions to see to the possibility of simultaneously financing or cofinancing bridging, redemption, and new funds transactions with the regional development banks of each area.

# IV. Financing Development, New Incoming Money, the New Regional Common Markets

## A. Financing Development

*1. Transfers between the rich countries and underdeveloped countries.*

    a. Up until 1983, the less developed countries did benefit from net transfers of financial resources. Ever since, there has been a drastic trend inversion: towards the late eighties, almost $40 billion were transferred to the industrialized countries.

    b. In such a manner, the transfers arising from the development aid on behalf of the industrialized countries are completely compensated, and lastly, a negative balance emerges at the charge of the less developed countries, which exceeds in cash terms and is much higher on an accounting basis.

    c. Serious foreign-debt problems are very likely to occur again if aid to development remains blocked at the actual modest percentages. There is a serious need for extra financings for the IFIs (World Bank and IMF) and requirements for greater financing and expansion of regional banks for development and their frame of action. There is a greater urge to help the average-income countries which previously ran or could run into grave indebtedness problems, and greater need to give financings to the low-income countries that haven't yet run into such problems thanks to their economic wisdom and capacity for managing their budgets.

    d. Besides, it is right to proceed according to the principle that only those making efforts of their own to solve problems—whenever possible and with the resources from their own taxpayers—deserve to be helped. The expression "whenever possible" should not have us overlook respect for fundamental human rights, which are the basis of civility at the foundation of our democratic actions.

e. Obviously, adopting these principles to solve the above-mentioned problems involves increasing the GNP share of aid for development, gradually changing the actual 0.35 percent into a 0.75 percent, as the DAC has continued to express is necessary in its government meetings. With a 0.7 percent figure of development aid, it is possible to obtain another sum equal to $40 billion; and should a fraction of such sum be used to produce an interest rate of aid to some LDCs, the possibility of obtaining further funds for these countries would be greatly increased. A possible explanation could be that 0.1 percent of the actual GNP of the creditor countries is expected to correspond to about $16.5 billion in 1991. If 1 percent of this sum were used for interest benefits, $30 billion could be made available for further financings.

## 2. *An international constitution of the public debt.*

a. True public debt cannot be financed through bank loans, given that information about the exact sum must be made available. Public debt must be constituted with negotiable securities. Moreover, issuing of public debt, at the international level, must be subjected to limits, based on objective parameters, which will help avoid the repetition of past pathologic phenomena. Also, the possibility should be explored of assigning revenues coming from particular tax measures in order to fight the debt problem.

b. There is another very different case in which the debt is contracted by a country and does not concern its budget on the whole, but specific investment projects. In such a case, it will be necessary to compare the financial profitability of the project to the collective economy. If there is a collective economy but there isn't financial profitability, issuing of international debt, even through shares at market conditions, appears to be a very risky formula for a country with a weak tax system, even if endowed with a good exporting capacity.

c. It is necessary, in this frame of mind, to widen the role of the regional development institutions, with concessionary formulas, as the ones used by Japan's Overseas Economic Fund, with a long duration period, low rates, and a greatly advantageous tolerance period.

## B. New Financing

*1. A few innovative instruments of new finance.*

a. Innovative finance transactions, which would receive the flow of private financing to the LDCs, including the East European countries, can be divided into two groups:
   (1) project financing
   (2) commodity financing

b. The first group of transactions concerns investment projects that are carried out and produce an income handled by operators from industrialized countries. The most interesting formulas are the BTO (build transfer operate) and the BOO (build own operate). Both come up with a foreign operator for management and offer the advantages of exporting technical and management know-how, and have an only partner.

c. The second group of transactions involves foreign investors' financing on specific exportations of enterprises from the developing countries.

d. The most interesting example is the merchant banks. In this case, the service which is rendered by the foreign bank to the LDCs enterprise does not only involve credit, but also technical assistance, which is necessary to obtain an exportable product and is particularly useful in international trading. This way, even the very small enterprises of the LDCs can manage selling on the big international markets.

e. One financial instrument that is definitely appropriate for the LDCs is that of commodities bonds. These bonds, even though providing for the repayment of the capital amount subscribed and the payment of interest coupons during the life of the bonds, are tied to a parameter of reference by means of a mechanism which can vary the value of the principal amount as well as the interest coupons. Such a parameter of reference is usually the price of a "commodity," that is, of a "base merchandise" or "raw material" of which the debtor country is an exporter.

f. The function of the reference measuring system and that of the guarantee stock could also be performed with nonmining raw materials, such as wood, or nonperishable farming goods, such as cereals. If efficient measures and conditions of guarantee are achieved, through the adequate legal elements and deposit space, all these commodities could generate these bonds.

## 2. Direct investments.

a. Direct investments can take various shapes in the collaboration with private and public economic forces of the less developed countries. An international enterprise can either be entirely foreign or partly financed by local economic operators. It can also, with the public enterprise of an LDC, turn into a mixed economy (this is also true for the European East) or it can take the shape of a joint venture between operators of the two geographic areas.

b. In an enterprise where capital with voting rights is entirely foreign, there can be forms of collaboration with domestic capital through bonds which are convertible into stock shares.

c. These various formulas have a particular interest in offering repatriation opportunities for capital invested abroad. This is a very delicate topic, which we leave in the hands of the governments of the developing countries. These should evaluate all the touchy tax problems which could be brought out.

d. Joint ventures between national private operators and foreign operators seem particularly appropriate for small and medium enterprises.

3. *The new regional common markets.*

a. The Uruguay Round's outcome is still very uncertain. If particular points being discussed by all are not resolved, there could be strong tension in trading within the group of industrialized countries as well as between the industrialized countries and the developing countries. This is why it's important that the talks have a positive outcome.

b. At the same time, it appears to be advantageous to focus on the development of regional areas of "common market," each being shaped according to local requirements and characteristics. The recent project concerning free trading areas between the U.S.A. and Mexico offers good prospects; more, similar projects should be undertaken.

c. The time of the large regional areas has come. There will be a much easier solution to the debt of Latin America, Africa, and Asia if with the "new money" there are also "new areas" of common market in each of these continents, between industrial countries and LDCs (PMA) which belong to the same large region. The principal aim of these trading groups naturally should be that of encouraging world liberalization of trade.

# V. Suggestions for Regional Areas and Groups of Countries

## A. Mediterranean and Sub-Saharan Africa

*1. The intermediate countries of Mediterranean Africa.*

    a. The problem of the African debt—approximately $250 billion—is divided in two parts: that of the countries of Mediterranean Africa (about $105 billion) and that of the countries of Sub-Saharan Africa (about $145).

    b. The debt of the Mediterranean countries concerns countries which are officially classified as average-income countries because they go beyond $545 per capita; their income goes from a little less than $700 in Egypt to a little more than $830 in Morocco, to about $1,200 in Tunisia and $2,400 in Algeria.

    c. Instead, countries like Egypt, Morocco, and Tunisia are classified by the World Bank as low-to-average-income countries. In my opinion, the very industrialized countries should acknowledge the existence of this category as one different from the average-income countries, for purposes of lightening the debt burden and granting new financial means for economic and social growth.

    d. All this involves an expansion of the list of the countries benefitting from the Toronto Plan and adapting this program to the greatest requirements. It also contains particular viewpoints on development aid bilateral policies.

*2. The Mediterranean bank for development and new financing.*

    a. Debts and development of Mediterranean African countries are a problem of common interest for Europe and Africa. A regional bank for development, able to work like the Interamerican Development Bank (Italian text: Banca Interamericana di Sviluppo) and Japan's "Overseas Development Corporation," is indispensable to direct towards these countries new financial resources for infrastructural investments and to support—through insurance guarantees and cofinancings—productive investments.

b. For the average-income countries like Algeria and Libya, the main problem concerns the new financings as well as the granting by the public insurance companies and banks of the industrialized countries (especially the European countries) of the new, innovative financing formulas.

3. *Cuts on official debts for the intermediate countries.*

a. There are greater problems for Morocco, Tunisia, and especially Egypt, as the greatest part of their debts are contracted with governments and the IFIs. A part of the Egyptian debt—$50 billion—is a military debt contracted principally with the U.S.A. This is an unusual case which requires a very particular and highly concessionary solution.

b. Generally speaking, it would be a good idea to carry out a substantial reduction of public credits or credits with bilateral public guarantee of the average-income countries, giving a thirty-year payment term, curtailing interests up to 60 percent and committing a quarter of the remaining sum to environmental protection, human capital formation, childhood and development. I would give particular attention to environmental plans concerning the Mediterranean area and to professional training programs for the emigrant work force.

4. *Recovery policies.*

a. It is fundamental to bring about the internal recovery policies in a firm manner. It is indispensable to carry out improvements of public income and to eliminate and modify a significant number of corporative dirigism regulations and forms of collectivism and paracollectivism, focussing on a strong modernization of the market structures and emphasizing the poorest category of the population's needs.

b. The sub-Saharan African debt now amounts to $145 billion. For the poor countries, the full payment of these interests and liquidations—given the total absence of economic growth and exportation—implies sacrifice on basic necessities, and raises the tragic and irremediable question: should the industrialized countries cut on the already low investment or should they reduce furnishings of essential consumption goods, which are already generally below the survival level?

c. In sub-Saharan Africa, in the 1980–86 period, because of the weight of these loans the gross product went down 3.1 percent per capita, while consumptions dropped 2.4 percent and exportations went down 2.1 percent annually in real terms, while importations dropped 7.5 percent annually, thus cutting all together new investments, consumption and maintenance. Growth was also affected by the repeated natural disasters.

d. In spite of the overall flow of resources, thanks to the unsecured aid and the bilateral and multilateral loans that constituted 7.0 percent of the GNP, there was a disastrous decline of capital accumulation, which from 20.2 percent of the GNP in 1980 passed to 11.4 percent in 1984, and went back up only slightly, to 15.9 percent, in 1987.

e. We can now say that, without any drastic cuts on these countries' debt, the economic problems of sub-Saharan Africa cannot be solved.

## 5. *Official creditors' remission of the debt for poorest countries.*

a. For the poorest countries—IDA eligible—according to what was decided by Italy and France, a political, economic, and ethical duty compels one to proceed to cancelling these debts' service, without affecting other financial aid.

b. For what concerns the bilateral creditors of noneligible poor countries, it would be a further step to manage converting the loans into credits with a forty-year liquidation period at an extremely low interest rate of 1%; its service would go to counterpart funds in indexed local currency to finance development projects, the environmental issue (such as the safeguarding of equatorial forests and fighting desertification) and human capital exploitation. For average-income countries, reductions should be less. Overall, $3.2 billion worth of interest could be "given back," while the remaining $800 million would go—like redemptions—to counterpart funds.

c. Five billion less of debt service, of which $3.5 billion is deducted from the public balances, and $750 million from the banks' and multilateral institutions' balances, makes little difference in the finances of the rich. And these sums mean survival for the poor, giving them the possibility of drawing more aid for that GNP growth of 6 percent which is considered possible and is indispensable. This target is possible; moreover, it's a duty on our part.

## B. Latin America and the Caribbean

*1. Transfers out of Latin America.*

a. Latin America is the only developing continent which, for almost a decade, has given a transfer of resources to the rich countries. The $10–11 billion net inflow in Latin America and the Caribbean of 1980 and 1981 has now turned into an "outflow" of $18 billion dollars in 1982, $31 billion in 1983 and so on, until the $25 billion "outflow" of 1989. This amount would have been quite higher if it hadn't been for the great accumulation of arrears.

b. Between 1982 and 1989, payments on interests and

redemptions went up to $350 billion, a figure equivalent to the earnings on exportations in a three-year period. A $330 billion debt grew to $435 billion in 1989.

c. The necessary surplus for the service of the foreign debt was principally obtained by means of the compression of importations through devaluations, monetary squeezes and reductions of investments and real salaries. Generally, the debt service was not financed by the balance, or it was only in a limited manner. It was financed through the monetary expansion while savings were transferred abroad.

d. The average rate of inflation of Latin America went from 57 percent in December of 1981 to 994 percent in December in 1989, with subsequent peaks beyond 3000 percent in Argentina, Nicaragua and Peru, while it was 1500 percent in Brazil and between 80 percent and 90 percent in Venezuela and Uruguay.

e. The picture wasn't all that dark, given that some countries like Chile and Mexico had manag to control terrible inflation. Besides, a number of countries were even able to return to a democratic system. Many more countries are now adopting less incoherent economic and fiscal policies.

## 2. *Debt and underdevelopment.*

a. Latin America and the Caribbean offer great resources, which haven't been properly exploited because of the burden of the debt service. In the 1980s, the gross product only went up 1.5 percent annually, and as a consequence the per-capita product went down 0.8 percent annually: almost 10 percent in a decade.

b. This situation is also due to the investments compression deriving from a huge financial drain. Nevertheless, the loss of growth cannot be measured only according to the capital that was lost. Any plausible explanation should include the deflationary gap, caused by the compression of internal demand brought about to generate commercial surplus, the negative effect on savings and productive accumulation due to the uncertainties of the financial horizon and to distorted policies. The lack of growth affected the paying capacity and set off this endless crisis.

*3. A recycling and reductions plan.*

    a. The issue on the debt and development in the Latin American and Caribbean region should become a permanent issue in the agenda of the G–7 and other donating countries.

    b. A reductions and recycling plan to relieve Latin America and the Caribbean from the crisis and place them in a condition to grow according to their own capacities must lie on solid bases.

    c. For a start, governments should carry out reductions and lightenings on the average-income countries' official debts, similar to the ones the commercial banks accepted for the Brady Plan. The program must also be reinforced through the conversion of a part of the debt service into counterpart funds, to be paid in indexed domestic currency, and intended for purposes of environmental safeguard, childhood, human capital, and growth. The suggestion just made about the African countries is also valid for the intermediate countries.

    d. Then, special elements similar to those adopted for the poorest countries, as well as slightly less advantageous conditions, should be examined for Latin America and the Caribbean.

    e. As a third thing, there is a need for public resources to finance the infrastructures and spur the "new money" initiatives.

    f. The fourth thing is the refinancing and reinforcing of the Brady Plan: Brazil, Argentina, Ecuador, Peru and Bolivia, which all belong to the intermediate category, certainly cannot be relieved of their burden with the Brady Plan, which contains conditions applying to Mexico, or negotiated proposals for Venezuela. It is necessary to encourge incentives for interest reductions and level the convenience of this option to that of capital reductions. In this frame of mind, it is necessary to consider the possibility for certain countries to have a part of the interests paid in indexed local currency warrants which can be converted at par into local property. Everything must be done to speed up the conclusion of the agreements and launch the "new money" option as well as "highly" advantageous financial means for the buy-back transactions, which, in certain extreme cases, seem the best solution, and in others can be one more option.

*Each country has to do its share.*

a. However, Latin American countries too must do their share. Governments must play a role by accepting the unpopularity of new taxes, because their external debt is—up to an extent—a domestic public balance deficit problem. Public bodies must make an effort in adapting to economic formulas which give the private sector more emphasis. The rich and middle class must contribute by investing in their own country instead of abroad. All must collaborate by paying their taxes and public fares, and by giving up populism.
b. Latin America's growth is a common interest for all of us, not only because of an international political, economic, and social equilibrium, but also because of the drug and migration issues.
c. After the lost decade of the eighties, citizens of Latin America and the Caribbean are entitled to a decade of progress in the nineties. They need our help, as much as they need to help themselves, in a context of constructive institutional cooperation.

## C. The East European Countries

### 1. *Two possible strategies for transition.*

   a. On the grounds of the considerations made in the first part, it is possible to make an outline of the strategic elements to face the debt problem in the East European countries. First of all, the strategies aiming to a debt reduction of these countries must avoid past errors.
   b. A rapid process of global transition must be fostered with financings at the level of enterprises. Public debt must be replaced with private debt and direct investment; it is important to encourage the use of innovative formulas focusing on new financial means, and tied to the accomplishment of investment projects and to the exploitation of raw materials, based on international trading collaboration.
   c. What is more important still is to examine the possibility of the "New East European Payment Union" linked to the EEC and its financial institution, speeding up a general convertibility, as was done after the war in Western Europe, with the help of the United States.

### 2. *The double purposes of our suggestions.*

   a. The outline here suggested has two important positive effects: first, it allows and facilitates development of financial and management autonomy of enterprises, and the flourishing of small and medium enterprises and development of the market system; second, it prevents the formation of new foreign public debt which would only be an ephemeral relief for the economy, making less likely the chances of obtaining credit and blocking financings to productive enterprises.
   b. Creating areas of free trade associated with the EEC, according to the political line of large regional areas, would be much more efficient than concessionary loans directed to the public sector.

## VI. A Series of Measures to Lighten the Debt of the Various Categories of Debtor Countries

The various suggestions mentioned up to now can be summarized as follows:
1. New forms of debt remission for the low-income countries (per-capita income not beyond $545).
   a. *Total remission of the debt service of aids credits for the "IDA only" countries.*
   b. *Conversion of the nonconcessionary bilateral debts into long-term credits, at IDA conditions.* Payments of these credits should be directed towards credits with an interest in indexed local currency, to finance development projects aiming at protecting the environment and at exploiting human capital correctly.
   c. *Expansion of the financial resources of the IFI's concessionary facilities.*
2. Reduction of the debt burden for the low and average income countries ($545–$1,300 per capita).
   a. *Conversion of bilateral public loans into thirty-year credits,* extremely concessionary and with interest payments to be used for the constitution of counterpart funds in local currency (as mentioned in 1b).
   b. *Reinforcing the Brady Plan for what concerns debts to commercial banks,* with greater available funds of the IFIs to facilitate aid on the interests and to ensure equality between reductions transactions on capital and interests. There should be other measures like "bridging" measures, buy-back financings, payments in indexed local money, and fiscal and accounting improvements in favor of the crediting banks committed to reductions and new financing transactions. The final target is to reduce the debt burden to 50 percent.
   c. *Increase of concessionary loans.*
   d. *Growth of the role played by regional banks,* especially of their facilities in concessionary terms.
3. Lightening for the average-income LDCs (from $1,300 to $6,000 per capita).

a. *Conversion of the nonconcessionary bilateral credits* mentioned under 1b.
   b. *Reinforcing the Brady Plan,* according to the procedures described under 2b.
   c. *Just as in 2c–d* but with less concessions.
4. Reductions for the East European countries in the transition phase.
   a. *Conversion of the nonconcessionary bilateral debts* (as under 1 b).
   b. *Applying the Brady Plan* (as under 2b).
   c. *Multilateral new money instruments* (BERS) to support the transition phase and the fast passage to a market economy and to launch infrastructural investments in some key sectors.
5. Enforcing all the instruments of new finance for all countries, especially when it comes to BOT and BOO or "commodity bonds" (to be complemented with public insurance guarantees).